Interlending and Document Supply
in Britain Today

CHANDOS
INFORMATION PROFESSIONAL SERIES

Series Editor: Ruth Rikowski
(email: Rikowskigr@aol.com)

Chandos' new series of books are aimed at the busy information professional. They have been specially commissioned to provide the reader with an authoritative view of current thinking. They are designed to provide easy-to-read and (most importantly) practical coverage of topics that are of interest to librarians and other information professionals. If you would like a full listing of current and forthcoming titles, please visit our web site **www.chandospublishing.com** or contact Hannah Grace-Williams on email info@chandospublishing.com or telephone number +44 (0) 1865 884447.

New authors: we are always pleased to receive ideas for new titles; if you would like to write a book for Chandos, please contact Dr Glyn Jones on email gjones@chandospublishing.com or telephone number +44 (0) 1865 884447.

Bulk orders: some organisations buy a number of copies of our books. If you are interested in doing this, we would be pleased to discuss a discount. Please contact Hannah Grace-Williams on email info@chandospublishing.com or telephone number +44 (0) 1865 884447.

Interlending and Document Supply in Britain Today

EDITED BY
JEAN BRADFORD
AND
JENNY BRINE

Chandos Publishing
Oxford · England

Chandos Publishing (Oxford) Limited
Chandos House
5 & 6 Steadys Lane
Stanton Harcourt
Oxford OX29 5RL
UK
Tel: +44 (0) 1865 884447 Fax: +44 (0) 1865 884448
Email: info@chandospublishing.com
www.chandospublishing.com

First published in Great Britain in 2006

ISBN:
1 84334 140 9 (paperback)
1 84334 188 3 (hardback)

British Library Cataloguing-in-Publication Data.
A catalogue record for this book is available from the British Library.

Typeset by Domex e-Data Pvt. Ltd.
Printed in the UK and USA.

Contents

List of figures and tables

Figures

Tables

About the authors

Jean Bradford is a graduate of London University and qualified as a librarian in 1974. She became the Librarian in charge of the Inter-Library Loans Section at the University of Bristol Library in 1977 after 3 years as a cataloguer. Since 2000 she has also managed the Serials Section and from 2002 the Binding Section. Jean is also responsible for copyright compliance within the University of Bristol Library. She has served on the Forum for Interlending and Information Delivery (FIL) Committee and was Treasurer of FIL from 2001 to 2003.

Jenny Brine is Supervisor of Interlending and Document Supply at Lancaster University. She has also worked at the School of Oriental & African Studies in London, the Centre for Russian & East European Studies in Birmingham, Robert Gordon University, Aberdeen, and the library of the Royal Lancaster Infirmary. She has been Secretary of FIL since 2003.

Neil Dalley is a Senior Customer Services Consultant at SirsiDynix. He previously worked at Reading University Library as Document Delivery Co-ordinator, responsible for the strategic management of interlending and document supply (IDS) services and day-to-day running of the Inter-Library Loans office at the Main Library. He was Secretary of FIL from 2000 to 2003 and Chair for 2003/04.

Jill Evans was the Inter-Library Loans Librarian of Edinburgh University Library prior to joining the National Library of Scotland as the Deputy Manager of Inter-Library Services. An appointment to the post of Project Manager for the Consortium of University Research Libraries (CURL) and British Library Monograph Interlending project gave her practical experience and knowledge of the UK and international lending communities to contribute to the work of the project. A recent FIL Committee member, Jill is currently the Service Development Manager of the Scottish Confederation of University and Research Libraries with liaison responsibilities for the development of consortial projects and initiatives.

Marian Hesketh is a graduate of Manchester University and qualified as a librarian in 1977. She has worked in the Requests section at Lancashire County Library Headquarters since 1989 and has been responsible for IDS borrowing in the county since 1992.

Tracey Jackson is Inter-Library Loans Manager at Hertfordshire Libraries. She has worked at Hertfordshire Libraries since 1988, moving from the Central Stocks Unit to the Central Resources Unit and finally to the Inter-Library Loans Department. She is currently the FIL Membership Secretary.

Betty Lowery is currently Customer Services Manager for the British Library's Document Supply Services. A graduate in French, she obtained her professional library qualification from Loughborough School of Librarianship and began her career working as a cataloguer at Leicester University. For the last 21 years she has been working at the British Library in a variety of posts, within both Operations and Marketing, and has been Manager of Customer Services for the last 11 years. She attends all FIL Committee meetings as an observer.

Stephen Prowse is the Journals/Document Delivery Co-ordinator at King's College London. He has worked with Ex Libris on development of the ILL module of Aleph and recently served on the steering group of the CURL/British Library Monograph Interlending project. He is a past chair of FIL and a regular contributor to the journal *Interlending & Document Supply*.

Penelope Street is Faculty Librarian for Medicine and Veterinary Science at Liverpool University. Previously, she was Head of Serials and Inter-Library Loans at the University and a past Secretary and Vice Chair of FIL. She is currently Secretary of the International Federation of Library Associations Section for Document Delivery and Resource Sharing.

The authors may be contacted care of the Editors:

E-mail: *j.i.bradford@bristol.ac.uk*
      j.brine@lancaster.ac.uk

Introduction

Jean Bradford

This book grew out of a Roadshow organised by the Forum for Interlending and Information Delivery (FIL). The event was organised for newcomers to interlending and document supply (IDS) and the organisers wanted to produce a reading-list for delegates so that afterwards they could find out more about the topics presented on the day. Although there were numerous articles of relevance to their work, they could not find a book about the IDS system in the UK today. This book aims to fill that gap.

All the authors are librarians with experience in IDS. We aim to cover the topics which are most relevant to the work of IDS practitioners in the UK. We also look at wider issues, so that IDS can be seen in context. This should be useful to people who are responsible for the day-to-day work of IDS, and also enlighten those who manage the service and need to understand the challenges that IDS brings, and plan for change. IDS has often been referred to as the 'Cinderella' of the library world. In recent years it has come to the fore, as libraries, faced with the ever-increasing cost of serials subscriptions, have looked to 'access' rather than 'holdings' to supply their users' needs. This book is therefore timely. It includes a description of current practices and issues together with a look at the future. We hope that it will also help librarians in other countries, where the organisation of IDS is very different, to understand UK practices better. The focus of this book is the UK IDS system. Other countries have different models, but we have not attempted to describe them or to compare the UK system with them.

Throughout, IDS is used as the term to refer both to loans supplied between libraries and to the supply of copies of articles no matter what format that copy may take. The British Library Document Supply Service (BL) occupies a central place within the UK system for IDS and so a whole chapter is devoted to it. A glossary of other frequently used terms is provided at the end of the book.

Libraries in every sector are involved in IDS and each sector has its own priorities. We have included a chapter about IDS in a number of different organisational settings and we hope that this will enable the reader to understand better the particular needs of other libraries. There is also a chapter about co-operation. IDS is often the most tangible result of co-operation between libraries. However, co-operation brings wider issues that impact on IDS and the chapter aims to explore some of these issues.

Users in all libraries require a huge range of different bibliographic information. This can be very daunting – you can feel that you do not know where to start when faced with a request for an obscure report or a request in a language you have never encountered before. This is why there is a chapter devoted to all forms of bibliographic information.

Technology is important for IDS and so there are two chapters concerned with the application of information technology. One concerns the systems available to manage the IDS function and the other the systems which are now becoming important for information discovery and delivery. The aim of these two chapters is to explain the principles of these systems, not to recommend any particular product.

One chapter focuses on copyright for IDS practitioners, as it is vital to know what can be copied legally. We are very grateful to Charles Oppenheim of Loughborough University for reading through the draft of this chapter, and for his advice.

It is often said that staff are our most important asset, but this cliché does contain an important truth. People working in IDS need to keep in touch with each other, and keep up with recent developments, so one chapter looks at membership organisations, journals and abstracts. Staffing and training issues are discussed in the chapter on the IDS Department, which also looks at essentials such as workflow, costing, standards and statistics.

We are living in a world where national boundaries are increasingly unimportant when it comes to finding information. Our users expect to be able to have what they need regardless of its origin, so being able to approach libraries abroad is very important. The chapter on international IDS aims to explain how to do this. We must also remember that libraries from all over the world expect to be able to ask us for loans and copies, so this is not one-way traffic. We must make sure that we have systems in place to respond to their requests.

It is fitting that this book is the result of the work of several IDS librarians. Much of IDS work relies on the help and support that IDS staff in every institution give to each other. Co-operation and collaboration are the hallmarks of IDS, and it is this which has enabled this book to be completed. We are grateful for the assistance we have received from FIL, in particular financing our meetings and library visits. On behalf of myself and Jenny Brine, my fellow editor, I would like to thank all involved in this project for their hard work and enthusiasm.

The history of interlending and document supply in the UK

Jenny Brine

People working in Interlending and Document Supply (IDS) in the UK today are used to the British Library (BL) playing a central role in the system. However, the BL – or rather its antecedent the British Museum Library (BML) – played no part in the early development of IDS services. Some informal lending of books from one library to another undoubtedly took place in the 18th and 19th centuries, but it was 1916 before the first components of the complex system we know today were put in place.

Individual public libraries were under pressure from the growing demands of adult learners, whether in formal educational classes or self-educated. The Central Library for Students was set up using money from the Carnegie UK Trust, and began buying books to lend to other libraries, creating a union catalogue of books, and establishing links with specialist libraries willing to act as back-ups. In 1931 it was given funding from central government and public libraries and became the National Central Library (NCL). At the same time, public libraries began to band together to create regional library services, most of which created their own union catalogues. The universities had informal borrowing and lending arrangements between themselves; some would supply books if requested by the NCL. In 1937 the first union catalogue of university periodicals was published, which greatly facilitated interlending. Those working in science and technology were able to make use of the lending services of the Science Museum Library (SML) from 1924, while industrial and commercial libraries began to form city-wide groups in the 1930s, usually based on a major public library.[1]

After World War II, the provision of scientific and technical information to the UK's industries and businesses became a serious issue.[2] The creation of a National Lending Library for Science and Technology (NLL) was first proposed in 1949, and by 1956 the Department of Scientific and Industrial Research's London Lending Unit (LLU) was operational, under the iconoclastic metallurgist Dr Donald Urquhart. He wanted a library run by scientists, for scientists, and was famously impatient with conventional library techniques such as union catalogues. In 1961 the NLL opened at Boston Spa in West Yorkshire, with all the stock of the LLU and the lending stock of the SML. It soon became extremely popular, with use exceeding even Urquhart's expectations. The NLL's procedures were closer to those of industrial warehouses than those of conventional libraries, and it was at the forefront of innovation in areas such as the use of the telex, using computers to process requests, and producing bibliographies based on its huge collections of reports and conference literature. The NLL did recognise, however, that it could not provide a comprehensive collection of foreign-language literature and so set up reciprocal arrangements with the Technical University in Hanover for German items in the 1960s, followed by a similar agreement with the Lenin Library in Moscow.[3] These links eventually evolved into the BL's World Wide Search service. The initial focus on science and technology was soon diluted by the addition of clinical medicine and the social sciences.[4]

The 'Parry Report' of 1967 highlighted the effects on university libraries of the absence of a national library system.[5] The speed and efficiency of the NLL's services contrasted with the rest of the interlending service then available, particularly for the arts and the humanities. At the same time, world publishing output was increasingly very rapidly, particularly in medicine, science and technology. The government recognised that the continued economic, cultural and social development of the country needed a faster, more efficient library and information system. And so in December 1967 the National Libraries Committee was set up under the Chairmanship of Dr Frederick Dainton. The Dainton Report was highly critical of existing IDS services, commenting:

'the many different library and information services do not at present form a well-ordered pattern of complementary and co-operating parts, ... There is little machinery for assisting the co-ordination of even national facilities in closely related subject areas, for ensuring adequate coverage of material and bibliographical services, and generally for making the best use of available resources of all kinds.'

It was particularly critical of the lack of any co-ordination and co-operation between the national bodies it surveyed. The Committee recommended the creation of the British Library, with the BML becoming the National Reference Library for the UK and the NLL its lending service, renamed the British Library Lending Division (BLLD). The NCL was to become part of the BLLD. There were many other proposals, and IDS staff were particularly interested in the expectation that the BML would allow more of its stock to be copied, and a recommendation that lesser-used non-British material be available for loan to other libraries.[6] Most of Dainton's recommendations were accepted, and the new British Library came into existence in 1973.

The BL's first decade can be seen as a period of integration and computerisation.[7] At BLLD, innovations from that period which lasted until the end of the century included the development of the three-part request form and the XYZ search system, where X meant a stock search, Y stock plus locations and Z an overseas search. The ARTTel automated requesting service began in 1981. Problems with the cost and reliability of the postal service meant that the BLLD had to set up a transport system, using a combination of rail transport to major regional centres and vans provided by the local regional library services (RLSs). Boston Spa also acted as a hub for loans between regions. The NCL's union catalogues were maintained for a time; some such as the Slavonic Union Catalogue are still consulted today. Older books recorded in the catalogue of the NCL's own collection have now been incorporated into the British Library's Integrated Catalogue (BLIC), but some more recent material is still to be added. The 'back-up' system created by the NCL was refined to include all the copyright deposit libraries[8] and special collections such as of the Linnean Society and the Royal Society of Medicine. The BL sent requests direct to 15 major libraries; an additional 24 'special source libraries' could be approached by requesting libraries.

Nationally, it was a period of increasing economic restraint for the public sector, moving into recession by the end of the decade. The 1974 reorganisation of local government, which saw the amalgamation of many library services, encouraged the RLSs to rethink their activities. Their union catalogues were transformed by the introduction of COM – Computer Output in Microform. This was used to produce lists of International Standard Book Numbers (ISBNs) with locations attached, which greatly facilitated interlending of recent books. In this – as in many aspects of ILL automation for the public library sector – London and South Eastern Library Region (LASER) was a pioneer.[9] For libraries in universities, the Atkinson Report[10] of 1976 introduced the concept of the 'self-renewing library',[11] stimulating a debate in libraries about the importance of holdings versus access.[12] Library automation proceeded rapidly, with the creation of cooperatives such as Birmingham Libraries Cooperative Mechanisation Project (BLCMP). The automation of IDS systems lagged behind, partly because of the efficient paper-based systems run by the BL, and partly because of the service's low priority in many libraries. There was increasing interest in the provision of videos and other non-print materials though IDS. Fax machines became widely available, and photocopiers came down in price. Improvements in photography and printing resulted in the production of many more catalogues and union lists in printed form, either as computer printout or as photographs of library card catalogues. The first attempts to create a UK Library Database System – in effect, a national union catalogue – began in the 1970s, but foundered because of a lack of political will and investment, the high cost of computer power at the time and insufficient standardisation.[13]

During the 1980s and 1990s, however, the dominance of BLLD in the inter-library lending system came under increased scrutiny. As the public sector was forced to become more cost-conscious, customers began to consider whether they could get what they wanted more cheaply from elsewhere. The prevailing political climate fostered suspicion of public-sector monopoly and encouraged competition, so there was an 'ideological edge' to some of the explorations of alternative interlibrary loan provision.[14] The new BL building at St Pancras was the focus of much of the BL's attention for two decades; it not only required huge capital expenditure but also reduced management attention to other areas of the BL's work. Nevertheless, there were a number of significant advances in IDS, such as the introduction of Replies Intrays and the ADDAddress facility. Budgetary pressures on the BL throughout the period led to the cancellation of many serial titles and reduced book purchases. The policy of 'common stock' was developed in response to these pressures, with the aim of reducing duplication between London and Boston Spa.[15] In 1996/97 the acquisitions budget for the Document Supply Centre (DSC) was cut heavily, with foreign-language material suffering particularly. It was as a result of this that the BL began to allow some books to be borrowed from St Pancras. The BL catalogue became accessible to universities through JANET in 1993, and in 1997 the British Library Public Catalogue (BLPC) went online over the Web free-of-charge – but only after the BL had enraged the library community by suggesting that it might only be available for payment.

Beyond the BL, online services such as Dialog and Datastar – albeit often expensive and difficult to search – made users far more aware of the huge amount of literature available. Later, the widespread use of CD-ROMs for databases and union catalogues, which had previously been only available in paper form, prompted a rapid rise in requests for articles through IDS in the 1980s and early 1990s. Nationally the overall demand for IDS services peaked in 1997–1998. As the volume of work increased, and computers became cheaper and more accessible, the automation of IDS processes won more attention, both from library management system providers and from stand-alone developers. IDS work was made easier by rapid improvements in communications during this period, with most higher education (HE) libraries able to use email to send and receive requests by the mid-1990s.

The needs of disabled people were moving up the political agenda, and visually impaired users received more attention in IDS with the creation of the first union catalogues of alternative format materials (later to become RevealWeb). IDS provision of materials in ethnic minority languages was also given more attention.

The founding of the Forum for Interlending in 1988 can be seen as the 'coming of age' of the IDS professional, keen to assert independence from both the RLSs and the BL. There has never been a government organisation with overall responsibility for IDS across all sectors of library and information work, and FIL has provided an opportunity for practitioners to discuss issues, recommend good practice and be consulted by the BL.[16]

From the mid-1990s, the document supply scene in the UK was heavily affected by the availability of journal articles online. Many libraries in HE and industry subscribed to 'big deals', which included a huge number of lesser-used titles that in the past would have been the preserve of IDS. In addition, some scholars began to place their articles with journals that make them available free-of-charge to end-users; this trend too has reduced conventional IDS requests.[17] In the HE and further education (FE) sectors, the Follett Report of 1993 encouraged a number of projects affecting IDS. Some of these sought to find alternatives to the BL as a source of journal articles. The eLib programme funded a large number of electronic document delivery projects, such as LAMDA, EASY and DOCUSEND.[18]

There has been a rapid downturn in overall IDS activity in the UK since 1998–99 (see Figures 2.1–2.4 at the end of this chapter). This appears to have been largely due to alternative sources for journal articles; requests for loans of books are still buoyant. The BL has responded to changes in the IDS market in a number of ways, including introducing differential pricing for loans and copies, charges for location searches and phasing out paper request forms. The introduction of scanners has allowed it to compete with e-journals by offering Secure Electronic Delivery.[19] However, there is concern that if commercial e-journal suppliers 'cherry pick' the easy requests, it may become the 'library of last resort', rather than the 'library of first resort', which it was in the 1970s and 1980s. The BL continues to supply a significant proportion of the books and other materials lent through the IDS system, and performs a central role in the UK IDS system through its 'banker function'.[20]

The 1996 reorganisation of local government in England, Wales and Scotland caused an upheaval in IDS in public libraries. At the end of the decade changes in regional administration in England and Wales and the creation of the Museum and Libraries Archives Council (MLA)[21] resulted in a large-scale reorganisation of the RLSs; whereas some emerged stronger and more inclusive (such as Libraries NorthWest), others have struggled to find a new purpose.[22] After a period when the emphasis was on competition in the public sector, HE libraries have begun to work together on access agreements such as UK Libraries Plus and SCONUL Research Extra. In many regions, all publicly funded libraries, irrespective of sector, are working more closely together and enabling readers to use their collections in person, rather than relying on IDS.

The availability of library catalogues and union catalogues online (especially COPAC) has transformed IDS work, making it much easier for staff to verify bibliographical data and identify possible lenders themselves. On the other hand, the hope of a national union catalogue has been greatly weakened by the rift between LASER and most other regional library services in the early 1990s over the ownership of bibliographical data, and other issues. This resulted in two competing union catalogues – UnityWeb and Viscount (now LinkUK).[23] COPAC became widely available at the same time as the BL back-up library policy ended in 2001. This led to some major collections being flooded with requests which they could not handle, while other libraries not on COPAC suffered a large drop in applications. The end of the back-up system also saw some collections unilaterally increasing prices, while cooperatives such as CONARLS and SILLR introduced a reduced charge for loans between members. The van schemes used by the BL and RLSs to transport books were replaced by commercial couriers and the Post Office; this has had an impact on the cost and reliability of interlibrary transport.[24]

The increased availability of library catalogues over the Web and the ease with which readers can search for information over the Internet has made library users expect access to more foreign material. This has led to a rapid growth in direct international lending, particularly between universities.[25]

The history of IDS in the UK over the last century does not provide a blueprint for the future; however, this brief account should help library staff understand how the service came to be as it is today.

Notes

1. Roberts, Norman (1984) 'Interlibrary lending in England and Wales 1900–45', *Interlending and Document Supply* 12(3): 87–94.
2. Jefferson, George (1984) 'Interlibrary lending in England and Wales from 1952', *Interlending and Document Supply* 12(4): 119–28.
3. Houghton, Bernard (1972) *Out of the dinosaurs: the evolution of the National Lending Library for Science and Technology*. London: Bingley, pp. 60–1.
4. *Op. cit*, pp. 46–51.
5. University Grants Committee (1967) *Report of the Committee of Libraries*. London: HMSO [The Parry Report].
6. It was 1996 before the former British Museum Library agreed to allow lesser-used recent foreign material to be borrowed by other libraries.
7. Jefferson, *op. cit.*
8. The copyright libraries are the British Library, the National Library of Scotland, the National Library of Wales, Trinity College Dublin, Oxford University Library and Cambridge University Library.
9. Jefferson, *op. cit.*
10. University Grants Committee (1976) *Capital Provision for University Libraries: Report of a Working Party*. London: HMSO [The Atkinson Report].
11. Soon nicknamed the 'self-destroying library'.
12. For the background to this debate, see, for example, Baker, David (1992) 'Access versus holdings policy with special reference to the University of East Anglia', *Interlending and Document Supply* 20(4): 131–7; Blagden, John (1998) 'Opinion paper: access versus holdings', *Interlending and Document Supply* 26(3): 140–4.

13. Smith, Malcolm (2002) 'The cycles of interlending', *Interlending and Document Supply* 30(1): 25–31.
14. Smith, *op. cit.*
15. See, for example, Wood, David N. (1992) 'Recent developments at the BLDSC', *Interlending and Document Supply* 20(4): 159–63.
16. FIL and other professional organisations are discussed in Chapter 5.
17. See, for example, Brindley, Lynne (2005) 'The British Library: its origins, development and future', *Interlending and Document Supply* 33(2): 76–80.
18. These are summarised in: Law, Derek (2005) 'Tilting at windmills: BLDSC and the UK higher education community', *Interlending and Document Supply* 33(2): 85–9.
19. Electronic document delivery is discussed in Chapter 9.
20. The British Library today is discussed in Chapter 3.
21. On MLA and regional organisations today, see Chapter 4.
22. The development of regional library services and the reasons for their reorganisation in the late 1990s are well explained in: Brewer, Stuart (2002) 'The regional perspective', In *Co-operation in action: collaborative initiatives in the world of information.* Edited by Stella Pilling and Stephanie Kenna. London: Facet, 46–66.
23. On union catalogues, see Chapter 7.
24. On transport, see Chapter 9.
25. International IDS is discussed in Chapter 12.

Figure 2.1   BLDSC demand, 1973–2001

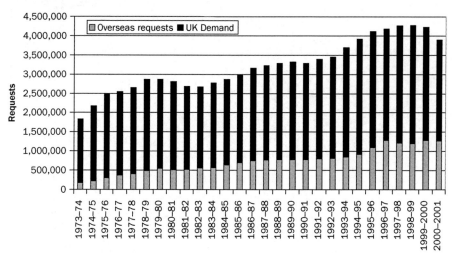

Source: British Library Document & Bibliographic Services, Facts and Figures April 2001, p. 2

Figure 2.2 IDS applications, higher education, 1993–2004

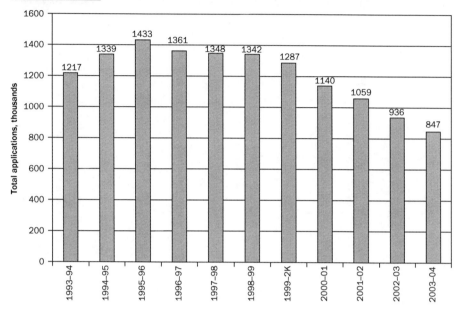

Source: LISU Annual Library Statistics 2004 and SCONUL Library Statistics 2003–2004

Figure 2.3 Public Library IDS activity, 1991–2002

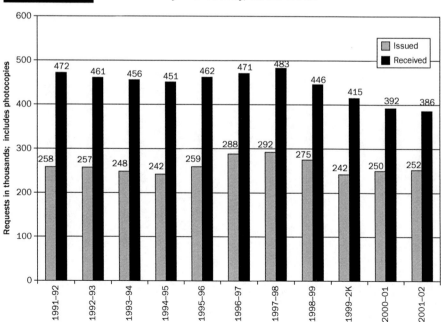

Source: LISU Annual Library Statistics 2003–2004, Table N

Figure 2.4 Governmental Departmental Libraries IDS activity, 1992-2003

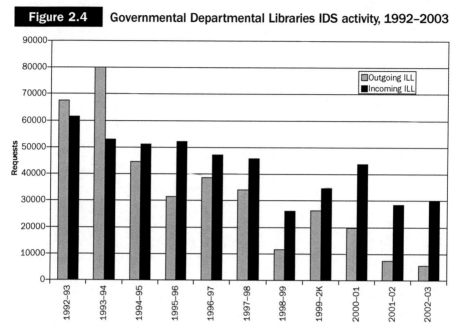

Source: LISU Annual Library Statistics 2004, p. 145

3

The British Library and document supply services

Betty Lowery

Introduction

The British Library (BL) is the world's leading document supplier. The Document Supply service at Boston Spa sits at the heart of the interlending environment in the UK, and anyone can have access to the vast collections of the BL through this service. Every day its Document Supply service receives thousands of requests from organisations and individuals both in the UK and overseas. Customers range from public libraries, universities, and businesses with research and development departments to individuals with specialist research needs. Requests are supplied for current, historical and international material, from 19th century art journals to German philosophy from the 1930s, from the latest nuclear research to articles from the early days of the 'Gentleman's Magazine'. Many of the UK's major pharmaceutical companies are dependent on the BL to keep them up to date with the latest research; through the service many health organisations learn about ground-breaking treatments in the medical field and even those who are only served by a fortnightly visit from a mobile library can still have access via their public library.

In 2003 the BL commissioned a research study to estimate the economic impact of the Library on the UK economy. The results of the study showed that the BL generates value around 4.4 times the level of its public funding or, to put it another way, if the BL did not exist, the UK would lose £280m of economic value per annum. Investment in the Library therefore pays huge dividends and represents value for money for the British taxpayer. This value is not only for those who access the collections and services directly, but also for those who receive the indirect benefits of the results of scientific research, creativity and innovation.[1]

The BL is constantly striving to improve its services. The first phase of modernisation of the Document Supply service was completed in 2003, when the BL negotiated partnership agreements with publishers and software suppliers to enable them to build the technical infrastructure needed for a new streamlined service. Hundreds of photocopiers were replaced with high-speed scanners and the Secure Electronic Delivery service was born. A quarter of items are now being delivered by this means and organisations are incorporating this into their working processes.

The collection

The BL's holdings can be divided into material which is available for loan, and the reference collections. Copies of all items published in the UK have to be deposited with the BL, and material in this legal deposit collection can never be borrowed. The Document Supply collections held in Boston Spa have to be purchased, so certain guidelines have to be followed to ensure best use of the acquisitions budget.

The Document Supply service at Boston Spa purchases 'worthwhile' literature of a reasonable academic standard to meet the needs of higher education, industry, commerce, the professions and research organisations. Its purpose is to supplement collections, rather than replace them, particularly in the case of public libraries. It does not collect fiction, textbooks, juvenile material or trade literature. In the case of serials, it collects extensively, irrespective of subject or language. For monographs, the material is predominantly in English, whether from the UK or US. It also has an extensive collection of conference proceedings, official publications (all Stationery Office publications as well as European Union material) and theses, together with much report literature, both in microform and in hard copy. Report literature comprises documents that contain results of research and development work, investigations and surveys, and can often be very difficult to trace, not being covered by the usual range of bibliographic tools and rarely available through normal bookselling channels. When sending requests for any material through the BL, it is always helpful to provide as much information as possible, but this is particularly true of report material, especially if you know an alpha-numeric code, as this could provide the vital clue to tracing the item in stock.

You can also obtain Slavonic material, cover-to-cover translations of Russian scientific serials as well as much other material in translation. The Document Supply service holds a Translations Index, so staff can quickly let you know if an English translation is available. With these and other harder-to-trace materials it is always possible to send a speculative request to the BL as, in most cases, experienced staff will be able to trace the material for you.

The British Library Integrated Catalogue

The British Library Integrated Catalogue replaced the British Library Public Catalogue in 2004, when the BL adopted Aleph as its cataloguing tool. It contains all the Document Supply and reference collections listed in its predecessors, but also extends to the Asia, Pacific and Africa collections, maps, newspapers and printed music. It includes records from the Register of Preservation Surrogates (material held in microform as part of the Library's preservation programme). The catalogue is the same for all users, whether readers visiting the reading rooms at St Pancras, individual non-registered customers or Document Supply-registered customers. When carrying out a search, you will find entries from all parts of the BL, but you can make a catalogue subset search to narrow down the entries to the Document Supply collection only.

Some Document Supply material is not recorded on the BL Integrated Catalogue. This includes most monographs from 1950 to 1970, music, Russian scientific monographs before 1989, official publications up to 1979 and anything termed 'Parliamentary'. Reports series are in the catalogue, but individual reports are not.

Using the Document Supply service

Setting up an account

Most libraries that have a regular need for documents register to use the BL's Document Supply service. There is no charge for registration and a form is easily downloadable from the Web. This allows you either to open a billing/invoicing account and pay monthly or to open a deposit account and pay in advance. Deposit account users have the cost of any material supplied debited from their account, and when they need to replenish their account they are prompted to do so by a proforma invoice. Whatever type of account is used, all customers receive a detailed statement of their use of the service each month.

At the point of registration, all customers are given a unique customer code and password, which gives access to the Library's automated ordering systems. The combination of customer code and password also identifies a customer on the Document Supply service's database, so that they do not have to keep quoting a delivery address for their documents. This code also identifies for the BL such details as method of payment, currency, default delivery method, whether loan facilities have been granted, commercial or 'public-funded' status and contact name.

Ordering documents

Most organisations now use automated methods for sending requests for material to the Library. For those who send several requests at one time, the main methods are ARTTel and ARTEmail. ARTTel is an online interactive system, whereby you connect to the BL's automated request processing system via the Internet using Telnet. Alternatively, you can email a file of requests using ARTEmail. For both these methods, the file of requests must be formatted correctly in order to be printed out onto individual request forms at the BL. In the academic community in particular, institutions will be using interlending software that will interface with one of these methods and will ensure correct formatting. If libraries do not wish to submit files of requests, there are other options available. ARTWeb is a simple online order form for registered customers, which provides drop-down menus for the various options available. In addition, anyone can search the BL's Integrated Catalogue free of charge; this lists over 12 million items in the Library's collections and, once an item has been found, there is the facility to link this with an online order. Those with Document Supply accounts can use the registered customer option and log on to the system with their customer code and password. If you cannot find an entry in the catalogue, it is worth filling in the blank order form provided, as staff can then fully check all holdings for you.

As the BL deals with thousands of remote orders every day, it is essential that there is an easy way of tracking individual requests, so each one is allocated a request number, either by the automated system or by the customer. Requests are printed onto barcoded forms when they arrive in the Library, and these are 'wanded' at various stages so the progress of each request can be monitored. Requests are also automatically matched against the holdings in the Document Supply collection and a shelfmark added to the record. This enables them to be automatically routed to the particular shelving area where items are held. Organisations do not, therefore, need to spend valuable time undertaking extensive checking for shelfmarks in advance, although this can be helpful if there is likely to be any doubt about a particular title, for example if there are several serials with the same title.

At the time a form is printed out, other specific requirements are added to it. Special codes indicate to the Document Supply service the level of search that you want the Library to carry out. A stock check is limited to the BL's collection available for document supply in Boston Spa and London; a location search means that, if an item is not held in the BL, information about other libraries' holdings will be provided. Full details of the libraries used as locations can be found in the online Directory of Library Codes.[2] If an item is not available in the UK and is out of print, the BL can search abroad using a Worldwide Search. This can be quite expensive and, in some cases, can take a long time, but it nevertheless does have a reasonably high success rate.[3] Codes are also used to tell the BL if you want the material to be delivered rapidly, and are prepared to pay extra for this service. Other codes allow you to state that microform is unacceptable, or let the BL know that you must have an item in English not a foreign language. Message keywords tell the BL if you are reapplying or chasing up the supply of an item you have previously requested, or asking for a renewal.[4]

Delivery of materials

The use of codes is particularly important when you are giving instructions about the way that you want the material delivered. Most items in the Document Supply collection are available for loan, so if you require a whole item, rather than a copy of an article or a chapter from a book, you will need to give the instruction 'LOAN' on the first line of your request or choose 'loan' from the drop-down menu if you are ordering using a Web form. Most requests, however, are for copies, and the Document Supply service offers several delivery options and turnaround times for these.

For many years, photocopies were made of material requested, and these were sent out by post. Recently, however, all photocopiers were replaced by scanners and, once your order has been received, the document is scanned and sent to you by mail, fax, Ariel or as an encrypted PDF file through Secure Electronic Delivery (SED). You choose the delivery method by means of keyword codes when you submit the requests. Your orders are normally processed within 48 hours of receipt, but 2- and 24-hour delivery options are always available. Recent upgrades to the systems at Boston Spa mean that all requests, for whatever service, can be sent by automated means and streamed directly to the areas where the items are held.

Most delivery methods are self-explanatory, but SED documents need some initial tests (by you or the end-user) to ensure that you are able to download them. You first need to download and install the full version of Adobe 6.0 or later and activate the Digital Rights Management function, as this will enable you to read the encrypted files. You then let Customer Services know the email address to which you want your documents sent, and you can test this link by opening and printing a test document. When you place an order and tell us that you want it supplied by SED, the BL will send you an email telling you that the file is ready to be collected. You then follow the link in the email and download your document. All documents are sent to the address that you give the BL when you register for the service, unless you tell them otherwise. The Alternative Document Delivery (ADD) address service enables you to have material sent to an address other than the one registered, so material can be sent straight to your end-users. In the same way, material can be sent to a different email address through SED, or you can simply forward the email when it arrives, as long as you do not click on the link first.

As well as choosing the delivery method, you also have to say if the item your reader orders is going to be used for commercial purposes, as a copyright fee will have to be paid in addition to the service charges. This copyright fee is publication-specific and is passed to the Copyright Licensing Agency to be distributed to publishers and other rights-holders. Copyright fees do not have to be paid for items on loan. If an item does not require payment of a copyright fee, the end-user has to sign a declaration form saying that they are not knowingly infringing copyright law. This has to be signed before the intermediary, usually the Interlibrary Loans Librarian, requests a copy from the BL.[5]

Monitoring the progress of your requests

The BL provides a regular report on the progress of your requests by sending you an 'Intray'. This lists your request numbers and tells you what action has been taken on your request. You can then update the information on your system, and send replies to the BL if needed.

Third-party interlending

If an item you require is not held in the Document Supply collection, you can ask for a locations search to be carried out on your behalf. Locations are libraries in the UK and Ireland that are listed in the Document Supply service's records as holding the item. The reply arrives in your Intray with the message 'LOC'. You are given the relevant library codes, which you look up in the Directory of Library Codes. You then apply direct to the library.

The Document Supply service will facilitate payment for these transactions, so that you can claim for reimbursement for items sent to requesting libraries. There is a claim form on the website that you can complete with your customer code, the request number of the item supplied and the amount you wish to charge. Many libraries use the BL scale of charges, although they are not obliged to do so. A credit will then be made to your BL account and a debit made from the requesting library's account.

If the BL asks you to supply a loan or a photocopy to a library based outside the UK, it will refund the cost of photocopying and/or postage.

Reading rooms

Most researchers, scholars and those in the interlending environment will be aware of the reading room facilities at the BL in London. What many may not know is that there is a reading room facility at Boston Spa that is open to anyone over the age of 14. Reference books, bibliographies, and many abstracting and indexing tools are available for consultation by visitors, and all of the material in the vast collection there is available for use. To make sure that items needed are not out on loan on the day of a visit, advance requests must be received five working days before the date required. On the day of the visit, further items may be requested, but there is no guarantee of availability. Customers may also not be aware that the BL's Sound Archive is available, by appointment, through the Northern Listening Service in the reading room at Boston Spa.

If an item that you require is only held in London and does not form part of the Document Supply collection, you can consult such material in the reading rooms at St Pancras. You would need to apply for a reader's pass, either in person or in advance by post, and you would not be able to take the item off the Library premises. These items form part of the national heritage collection, so the Library has a responsibility to the nation to protect the collection from any damage.

Research services

The BL has a team of subject specialists and information experts who have many years of experience in providing high-quality research services for all sectors and all types of organisations. They will conduct searches on your behalf in all fields of science, technology and medicine, social sciences, arts and humanities, as well as finding market, company and product information. They will find patent information, any legal and regulatory requirements, and any news in your field of research. They locate the information by online searching of specialist electronic sources not always available through conventional Web search engines and undertake desk research using the vast resources of the largest collection of research literature in the world. If you do not have the resources, time or skills to source material for your users, you could use this service to identify references that you can then order through the Document Supply service. Some concessions may be available by linking these two services.

Imaging services (reproductions)

Older printed books, manuscripts, maps and music cannot be obtained through the Document Supply service at Boston Spa, but the BL does provide a high-quality reproduction service across all areas of the collection, including the Oriental and India Office collections. The service can be accessed both by visiting the Library and remotely by completing a Web order form. The turnaround time is longer than the Document Supply service because of the nature of the material, but you are gaining access to the BL's unique collections of material. If you want to use the material to reproduce in a book or article for example, you will require separate permission to reproduce, which can be obtained from the BL's Permissions service. Similarly, you may need to obtain separate copyright clearance, as the usual Copyright Licence is not applied.

Non-registered/end-user access

Although most large organisations register to use Document Supply services, those who have only occasional use of the service are able to submit requests through BL Direct. This is a new service that makes it easy to find articles from a 5-year archive of the 20,000 most requested journals held in the BL. You do not need to register to search the database and you do not need to take out a subscription. When end-users find an article that they want, they simply enter credit card details and the item can be supplied within their specified timescale, even within as little as 2 hours.

Current awareness

ETOC and Zetoc

The Electronic Table of Contents on BL Direct (ETOC) can be used as a current awareness tool for registered users of the Document Supply service, as they can freely search the database, but without using this as their ordering mechanism. Alternatively, the UK Higher and Further Education communities (.ac.uk organisations), as well as the NHS, can use Zetoc, a more extensive current awareness service launched in September 2000. It is a joint venture with JISC and Mimas and provides free access to the BL Electronic Table of Contents database, comprising the 20,000 journals most requested from the BL, as well as around 16,000 conference proceedings published each year. It is updated daily, so users can keep up to date with articles in all areas of research.

This service also enables researchers to set up table-of-contents alerts for their selected journals, so that, each time a new issue of a journal appears, its table-of-contents information is emailed to those who have selected that journal for an alert. All articles are available through the Document Supply service.

Inside

Those customers who do not qualify to use Zetoc can subscribe to Inside. This integrates searching, alerting and ordering in the same way, and also facilitates the management of document supply budgets for researchers within an organisation.

Help and advice

Customer services

Although the Document Supply service has been simplified over the years, it may still appear daunting to those customers who are about to register or who have just registered for the service. Help is always at hand in the form of an excellent Customer Services department whose staff can give advice on any aspect of the service. They are all experienced members of the BL's staff who have worked in several areas of the Library. They hold customer clinics each year in various areas of the UK and also attend regional meetings, so you have many opportunities to get to know them.

Guidelines

Full descriptions of all services and full details of procedures are available on the BL's website. In the section giving customer information you will find handbooks, prices, a Directory of Library Codes, links to online requesting and information on all aspects of the services that have been outlined in this chapter.[6]

Notes

1. More complete details are available at: *http://www.bl.uk/pdf/measuring.pdf*
2. The *Directory of Library Codes* is on the Web at: *http://www.bl.uk/services/document/dlc1.html*
3. The BL's World Wide Search service is described more fully in Chapter 12.
4. This is explained more fully in the BL's *General Handbook*, which is on the Web at: *http://www.bl.uk/services/document/custinfo.html#handbooks*
5. Copyright is discussed more fully in Chapter 11.
6. The Document Supply Web pages are at: *http://www.bl.uk/docsupply*

4

Co-operation in interlending and document supply

Jean Bradford

Interlending cannot take place in a vacuum. Librarians who need to obtain items from other libraries need a structure, which gives them a code of practice and rules for communicating with each other. The aims of this chapter are to examine the organisational framework within the UK which supports interlending and document supply (IDS), and to explain the roles different organisations play.

Why is a framework needed?

- Libraries need to know who has got what, so that they can ask for a loan or copy. One of the first things that happens, when libraries agree to help each other, is the provision of information about the stock that the different partners own. More information about union catalogues and their use may be found in Chapter 7.

- There are costs in providing an IDS service to others; staff time and postage are the obvious costs, but there are others such as the computer system for recording the loan. If a copy of an article is being made for another library, there are similar costs – as well as a legal obligation to charge for the copy. Agreement about the way in which libraries pay each other for their IDS services facilitates the supply of items because each party to the transaction knows what to expect. It is important that the system for payment is kept as simple as possible. A description of the BL 'Banker function' and other payment schemes is included later in this chapter.

- Libraries which lend items to others expect the item to be returned. But what happens if an item is lost? This is why a code of practice providing rules for this and other situations is required. Within the UK, the most recent code of practice is that prepared by Libraries NorthWest (LNW), which can be found on their website.[1] This has been accepted by the Circle of Officers of National and Regional Library Systems (Conarls) and by the Forum for Interlending and Information Discovery (FIL). Conarls' own code of practice, *Interlibrary Lending – Common Standards for Best Practice*, can be found on its own website.[2] At an international level are the International Federation of Library Associations' (IFLA) *International Lending and Document Delivery: Principles and Guidelines for Procedure*. They were first agreed in 1954 and underwent a major revision in 2001. They can be found on the IFLA's website.[3]

- Interlending is becoming an increasingly international operation. Requests for help come to British libraries from libraries around the world. It is helpful if in each country there is a central point which can facilitate lending between the libraries within its borders and with those in other countries. In most countries this is one of the functions of the national library. There is a more detailed discussion of international IDS in Chapter 12.

What types of organisation exist?

IDS is one form of resource sharing. Because no library is able to satisfy all the information needs of its users, IDS has often been the main reason why libraries have joined together to help each other. However, there are other areas where collaboration has helped libraries to provide a more effective service to their users. Developments in areas such as reciprocal borrowing schemes or changes in collection management policies will have an impact on IDS operations. IDS librarians need to be aware of issues beyond their own day-to-day operations so that they can be prepared for the influence on their own practice such developments and changes may have. IDS librarians need two types of organisations. First, they require organisations which are concerned with the strategic direction of libraries in all sectors; it is essential that these include IDS within their remit. Unfortunately, there is no clear lead organisation for IDS, nor is it clear how such a leader could best gain support from libraries in all sectors. In a recent report, Kentwood Associates explained that the situation leaves a lot to be desired:

Because no single body or co-operative organisation is taking a national lead, a plethora of uncoordinated initiatives is underway within the interlending sphere. This is not necessarily a disadvantage but does risk duplication and unnecessary competition. There is, however, no strategic context for development to which there is broad agreement.[4]

Second, they require organisations which help them to solve problems in their day-to-day operations, and which enable them to communicate among themselves. Organisations which facilitate operational issues can contribute to strategic thinking. Indeed, it should be one of their major roles. If there is no agreement about leadership among the strategic organisations, it is difficult for operational organisations to contribute to strategic planning for IDS. It would be helpful if this situation was addressed, to enable both strategic and operational organisations to function more effectively.

I will begin by looking at the strategic organisations and then at those which are concerned with the day-to-day operations of IDS. The role of professional organisations in IDS is covered in Chapter 5.

Strategic organisations

Government departments

Responsibility for libraries is shared among more than one government department. The Department for Culture, Media and Sport (DCMS) is responsible for public libraries, while the Department for Education and Skills oversees libraries in education, i.e. in schools, colleges and universities. Health libraries come under the responsibility of the Department of Health. Libraries in commercial organisations are often isolated within their own firm, and if any government department is responsible for these special libraries it will be the Department of Trade and Industry. This scattering of responsibility at government level is not helpful to IDS librarians, who work in libraries across all sectors.

The Museums Libraries and Archives Council (MLA)

The MLA is the latest name to be given to a body which is charged with developing strategy nationally for libraries. It was formed in April 2000, under the name Re:source, from a merger of the Library and Information Commission and the Museums and Galleries Commission. It was also given responsibility for archives. Now known as the MLA, it is leading a number of major strategic initiatives. It states its mission as:

> The Museums, Libraries and Archives Council (MLA) is the national development agency working for and on behalf of museums, libraries and archives and advising government on policy and priorities for the sector.
>
> MLA's roles are to provide strategic leadership, to act as a powerful advocate, to develop capacity and to promote innovation and change.[5]

As well as initiatives for both museums and archives, the MLA has undertaken some important work for libraries. The People's Network is the ground-breaking project to link all public libraries to the Internet, with trained staff on hand to give help and advice. The MLA is also responsible for implementing Framework for the Future, the UK Government's 10-year strategy for public libraries. The initiative that will be of most interest to IDS librarians is the Wider Libraries initiative (WILIP), which demonstrates that the MLA is concerned with all kinds of libraries, not just public libraries. The final report of WILIP was published in November 2003, and has resulted in a strategic advocacy programme called Routes to Knowledge. The report and information regarding further progress on its recommendations can be found on its website.[6]

Co-operation through partnership is seen as the way forward. In some areas a regional MLA has been set up, for example NEMLAC, SEMLAC and SWMLAC. The MLA has published a leaflet setting out the purpose of these regional organisations.[7] The regional organisations are in the process of working out their relationship with the MLA, and the MLA itself is undertaking a strategic review. It has undertaken widespread consultations and further research on the regional agenda. This process is ongoing and latest information can be found on the MLA website.

The British Library (BL)

The BL has been involved in inter-library co-operation to some extent ever since it came into existence in 1973. As a result of its strategic review in 1998, it is now trying to work more closely with other organisations to develop strategies for collection development, preservation, access, bibliographic records, etc. Its Web pages include a description of its activities with different sectors[8] and provide a link to the National Forum for Information Planning and Co-operation (NFIP).[9] In particular, the BL stresses its interest in working more closely with regional MLAs and with higher education. Derek Law has published an interesting account of the BL's relationship with the higher education community during the last 25 years.[10]

Operational organisations

The best known organisation for IDS staff in the UK is the BL and for this reason Chapter 3 is devoted to it alone. Because of its central role, the activities of the BL have an impact on those of all the other organisations involved in IDS operations.

Regional Library Systems (RLSs)

England has been divided into seven RLSs; in Scotland, the National Library of Scotland fulfils the same function. In Wales there has been a succession of organisations. The Directors/Managers of the RLSs, representatives from the National Libraries of Wales and Scotland, the Irish Library Council/An Chomhairle Leabharlanna and the British Library form Conarls. This provides a channel of communication through which ideas may be shared and their development co-ordinated. A representative of FIL is a co-opted member of Conarls.

The RLSs came into existence from 1931 onwards. They immediately began creating union catalogues of the holdings of the libraries in their areas. As a result, they have built up large databases of locations primarily for monographs. Recently, they have invested in technology to maintain their union catalogues and to make them more widely available. Although their early function was to facilitate lending between their members, the RLSs have enlarged their role. They are engaged in a variety of special projects, such as NEWSPLAN concerned with the preservation of local newspapers. They are also responsible for facilitating the transport arrangements for loans between their members, the other regions and the BL.

In 1997 the government decided to set up Regional Development Agencies (RDAs) and the legislation establishing these organisations was passed in 1998. The RLSs along with other regional organisations were expected to have the same boundaries as their local RDA. The majority of them have had to change their boundaries to bring them into line with this decision. For example, the South West Regional Library System (SWRLS) lost Oxfordshire and Hampshire and did not gain any other area to compensate. As a result they lost a sizable amount of income. The changes needed in the regional library services because of government policy gave rise to a great deal of debate and resulted in an influential Conarls report, *Carpe Diem*.[11]

At present a number of initiatives and changes are taking place, but it is difficult for those outside each region to follow progress. There is no central source of information to help IDS practitioners to keep up to date. Conarls may be able to help with this and it is taking steps to update its website. This is welcome and IDS librarians will need to monitor this carefully.

A pattern is emerging whereby, in the newly defined regions, a strategic body is set up led by the MLA, as described above. Operational activities within each region are looked after in a number of ways depending on the needs and resources of each region. For example, LNW has a business unit which manages and leads the day-to-day business of interlending. By contrast, although SWRLS adopted a similar model, it has recently decided not to renew the contract for its business unit and is now discussing how operational activities will be managed in the future. Interlending activities within the regions have declined as libraries have relied upon the services of the BL. This has raised questions about the role of regional organisations. The regional environment is changing and new partnerships such as Co-East are being formed.[12] This is where a strong strategic lead would be helpful. Regional organisations need to have a clear agenda and match their operations to this agenda.

Library and Information Plans (LIPs)

The concept of LIPs was introduced in 1986 in the third report published by the Library and Information Services Council (England), referred to as FDL3.[13] LIPs were to bring together all the library and information services in an area. It was envisaged that LIPs would be a 'bottom-up' approach to planning and co-operation within their areas and that they would encourage organisations to replace informal arrangements with a more deliberately planned approach. It was hoped that local authorities would act as an 'honest broker' through their public libraries. In this way

LIPs would include a wide range of different organisations, many of which had not before been involved in information planning. It was realised that a framework for co-ordinating the work of LIPs was necessary, so that the concept could be promoted and those involved would be able to share their experiences. This is undertaken by NFIP, the National Forum for Information Planning and Co-operation.

LIPs vary greatly. Examples of successful LIPs include SINTO 2000 in Sheffield and HATRICS in the South West. Although the LIP concept was first proposed for organisations in a geographical area, it was extended later to subject groups. These 'sectoral' LIPs now include those for music, sport and the visual arts. Some LIPs are a combination of geographical area and subject.[14] There has been discussion about the future of LIPs, because some have been more successful than others. There have also been problems in funding their activities. Although some funding was available for the preparation of the plan, none was available for implementing it, and so implementation of the plan depended on the willingness of the members of the LIP to make resources available. This limited what LIPs were able to achieve. It will be interesting to see how their work relates to that of the RLSs.

Changing patterns of regional co-operation

During the 1990s there were a number of reports which encouraged co-operation among libraries. As a result libraries looked for ways to enhance what they do by joining with other partners. Academic libraries were stimulated into establishing co-operatives as a result of the Follett Report.[15] The M25 Consortium, Consortium of Academic Libraries in Manchester (CALIM) and Avon University Libraries in Co-operation (AULIC) were all formed around 1992, the same time as the publication of the Follett Report.

The 1994 local government re-organisation resulted in a greater number of smaller authorities, encouraging the formation of local consortia. New relationships are developing to make best use of technology, and enhance the libraries' services to their communities. In the South West there is the Foursite Consortium, which brings together South Gloucestershire, North Somerset, Bath and North East Somerset and Somerset. Co-East, which includes Bedfordshire, Essex, Cambridgeshire and Norfolk public libraries among its members, is another example.

There are consortia in other sectors also, for example among health libraries. Examples of these are the Library and Health Information Network Northwest (LIHNN) and the South West Regional Library and Information Network (SWRLIN).

These are all consortia which have as members libraries which belong to a single sector. One of the values of the RLSs and LIPs is that their members are libraries from all sectors. This is in danger of being lost with the recent changes. It is also why the WILIP initiative mentioned above is important. Another cross-sectoral initiative, which is still at a pilot stage, is INSPIRE. INSPIRE is funded to work with public, academic and national libraries, but is keen to work with libraries in any sector. More information is on the INSPIRE website[16] and this is definitely something to watch closely.

What do consortia do?

Getting started

Time and resources are required when libraries work together. All partners must receive a benefit for it to be successful and it is better to start in a small way with something that all can agree on, and not to be over-ambitious. The Consortium of University and Research Libraries (CURL) is an excellent example of this. CURL initially comprised seven members: Oxford, Cambridge, Edinburgh, Glasgow, Leeds, Manchester and London University libraries. These libraries all wished to introduce online catalogues and were especially interested in cataloguing retrospectively their historical collections. They decided to do this as a joint effort and share their catalogue records. By doing this they hoped to save money as books could be catalogued once and each library with copies could use the same record. JISC then provided funding for their project, on condition that what they were doing was offered to the wider higher education community. So the CURL reference service began and other university library staff could use the CURL database to order their own catalogue records or check bibliographical details. Now the service has evolved into COPAC, which is available to everyone over the Web, and the original seven members have been joined by another 22. CURL libraries have sought to encourage lending between themselves and have had several projects to achieve this. Most recently, CURL has joined with the BL to carry out a Monograph Interlending Project. The report of this project can be found on the CURL website.[17]

A similar evolution has occurred at the Foursite Consortium, where the need to purchase a new library management system led to other things, as Rob Froud, Librarian of Somerset County Library, explained in an email to me:

> Three of the new Unitary authorities (Bath and North East Somerset, North Somerset and South Gloucestershire) and Wiltshire County Council joined Somerset in a joint procurement exercise for a new [library management] system. From the outset Wiltshire was clear that their involvement in this collaborative effort would cease at the end of the procurement phase. The four authorities which were to become Foursite, however, had an open mind about a shared operation. At the end of the exercise the decision was made to select a single system with a combined catalogue. All Four services agreed to lend freely across borders, doubling the stock available to their users from 1m items to 2 million. Somerset hosts the computer servers and each authority is responsible for its own local hardware. The Consortium extended almost immediately to include the Acquisitions process and Foursite Bibliographical Services acquires and catalogues (where appropriate) materials for all four authorities. Foursite has since its formation jointly procured the supply of books, AV materials and Binding. It has been successful in bidding for DCMS Wolfson funding to automate its mobile libraries, to provide the web catalogue and 24/7 telephone renewals system. In 2005 the Foursite Consortium retendered for a replacement LMS in partnership with Bristol who are now joining what has become – for the time being – labeled Fivesite, but a new name will follow. Although the LMS will be shared five ways, again with an integrated catalogue, Bristol will maintain its own Bibliographical services operation.[18]

Access schemes and reciprocal borrowing

Another important activity is reciprocal borrowing. Either readers from each library can borrow at partner libraries or the libraries agree to lend free of charge to each other. Both CALIM and AULIC have done this. Among university libraries, the Society of College, National and University Libraries (SCONUL) has introduced national schemes to allow students and researchers to access and borrow from the libraries at other universities as well as at their home institution. A new development is for members of the public to have access directly to library services without entering a library. An example of this is the Wisdom Project in the South West, which aims to link together the online catalogues of eight public libraries using Z39.50.[19] Users of the participating libraries can search the catalogues of all the partner libraries and place requests directly for items. The item is then sent to the user's branch library. The project is moving into its second stage and will include additional libraries, and it is hoped that libraries in other sectors may join in the future. A similar scheme is also operated by the libraries belonging to Co-East. This model is one way in which interlending may develop in the future.

Other areas of activity

Some consortia share specialist staff, for instance those with foreign language skills. Others co-operate on technological developments. One of the best ways to co-operate is to share training programmes, as this may enable the partners to offer a wider range of training sessions than each individual library would be able to do on its own. Training is an area where significant cost savings are possible.

The level of activity in a consortium depends on the choice of the partners. Everyone in the group has to feel comfortable with what they will be asked to give and what they will receive. The most difficult area is collection management/development. Will you rely on Library X to collect in a particular subject area and expect your readers to use that, while you collect in other areas and welcome Library X's readers?

We need to remember that setting up a consortium and planning its activities take staff time and may need some money to get up and running. There is literature about the experience of those who have been engaged in setting up co-operative arrangements, both here and in the US. Some references are included in the list of suggested reading at the end of this chapter.

Charging schemes

Payment for requests is one of the functions identified earlier as a reason for needing organisations to support IDS. The BL has its own charges for its services and many libraries charge each other at the same rate as the BL. However, when the BL introduced different rates for loans and for photocopies, Conarls set up its own charging scheme. The rate charged for loans by those who have joined the Conarls scheme is lower than that charged by the BL. In addition, members of certain regional systems, such as LNW, have agreed much lower prices for supplying items to each other. Scottish libraries have their own charging agreement.[20] However, a few libraries charge more than the BL rate, including the University of London Library (Senate House) and Cambridge University Library.

The BL has undertaken to carry out a 'Banker function' for the UK IDS system. When any library sends a request to another library, it gives the number of its BL account and a reference number for the request. When the other library supplies the item, it sends the details of the account number, reference number and the amount it wishes to charge to the BL on a spreadsheet. The BL incorporates the charge into the invoice which it sends that library for its own services, and adds on a 10p handling charge to cover its overheads in administering the system. It does not matter whether the library concerned is charging at the same rate as the BL or not. The BL will place a charge on the requesting library's account in line with the instructions from the supplying library and post a credit on the supplying library's account. The reference number enables the requesting library to identify the charge being made on its invoice and take up any queries directly with the supplying library. This service has proved very successful, as it has enabled libraries to recover the cost of supplying items to each other simply, and the 10p handling charge is acceptable to all concerned.

Conclusion

This has been a brief overview of IDS co-operation in the UK. It is a fast changing scene where it is difficult to follow all the developments which are taking place. The websites listed below may help you keep up to date.

Suggestions for further reading

The British environment

The journal *Interlending and Document Supply* contains articles relevant to IDS and resource sharing in the UK and also reports experience in other countries, so is an invaluable source of information for IDS librarians.

Blunden-Ellis, John (1994) 'Looking to the future: the Consortium of Academic Libraries in Manchester (CALIM)', In *The New University Library: Issues for the 90s and Beyond. Essays in Honour of Ian Rogerson*, edited by Harris, Colin. London: Taylor Graham, pp. 45–54.

CALIM has now developed into The North West Academic Libraries (NoWAL) and more information about their current activities can be found on the NoWAL website at *http://www.nowal.ac.uk/* [accessed 1 July 2005].

Craig, Tina and Norman, Frank (2004) 'An Unlikely grouping? The vision of CHILL. Co-operation between independent health libraries in London', *Health Information and Libraries Journal* 21: 58–61.

Froud, Rob (1999) 'The benefit of Foursite: a public library consortium for library management systems'. *Program* 33(1): 1–14.

Howley, Sue and Stevens, Andrew (2004) 'Routes to knowledge', *CILIP Update* 3(1): 38–9.

Pilling, Stella (2001) 'Cooperation and partnership in the national library context: with special reference to the British Library', *Alexandria* 13(1): 35–42.

Pilling, Stella and Kenna, Stephanie (eds) (2002) *Co-Operation in Action: Collaborative Initiatives in the World of Information*. London: Facet Publishing.

A view from Ireland

McDermott, Norma (2003) 'Extending our reach: resource sharing in Irish libraries', *Interlending and Document Supply* 31(3): 192–200.

The United States

Library Trends 45(3): 1997. Special issue on resource sharing in a changing environment.

Williams, Delmus E. (2000) 'Living in a cooperative world: meeting local expectations through OhioLINK', *Technical Services Quarterly* 17(4): 13–32.

Notes

1. *http://www.lnw.org.uk/bu/bestpractice.htm*
2. *http://www.conarls.org*
3. *http://www.ifla.org/VI/2/p3/ildd.htm*

4. Kentwood Associates. *A Review of the Future of Resource Sharing and Inter-Lending for the Combined Regions and Talis.* November, 2004. *http://www.talis.com/products/unityweb/review_future.pdf* [accessed 1 July 2005], p.3.
5. *http://www.mla.gov.uk/* [accessed 19 March 2005]
6. *http://www.mla.gov.uk/action/wilip/wilip.asp* [accessed 18 June 2005]
7. *http://www.mla.gov.uk/documents/regional_leaflet.pdf* [accessed 19 March 2005]
8. *http://www.bl.uk/about/cooperation/cooperation.html*
9. *http://www.bl.uk/about/cooperation/worknational.html*
10. Law, Derek (2005) 'Tilting at windmills: BLDSC and the UK higher education community', *Interlending and Document Supply* 33(2): 85–9.
11. Circle of Officers of National & Regional Library Systems. *Carpe diem: seize the day. Modelling futures for library regions in a changing cultural environment. A report to RESOURCE: the Council for Museums, Archives and Libraires.* Information North, 2000. Library and Information Commission Research Report 38.
12. *http://www.co-east.net/*
13. Great Britain. Department of Education and Science. Office of Arts and Libraries. (1986) *The Future Development of Libraries and Information Services: Progress Through Planning and Partnership.* London: HMSO.
14. There is a list of all the different LIPs and their contact details at: *http://www.bl.uk/about/cooperation/pdf/nfipcontacts.pdf*
15. Joint Funding Councils' Libraries Review Group (1993) *Report* [Follett Report]. Bristol: Higher Education Funding Council for England.
16. *http://www.inspire.gov.uk/*
17. *http://www.curl.ac.uk/projects/Monographfinal.pdf* [accessed 14 May 2005]
18. Email dated 1 July 2005.
19. *http://www.bristol-wisdom-sw.net/cgi-bin/crxz/index.pl*
20. Details can be found at *http://www.nls.uk/professional/interlibraryservices/services/sillr.html*

5

Professional networking

Neil Dalley and Penelope Street

To work effectively within interlending and document supply (IDS) you need to communicate with your colleagues and learn about what they are doing. It is always easier if you do not work in complete isolation and are able to draw on the knowledge and expertise of others. You may be the only person dealing with IDS in your organisation, so it is useful to share your experiences and avoid making every difficult decision alone. Because so much of interlending depends on co-operation it is perhaps more important for IDS staff than for any other library professionals to build up relationships with staff working in other institutions both in the UK and overseas.

CILIP

CILIP (Chartered Institute of Library and Information Professionals) is the overall professional body for staff working in an information environment. You can become a member whether or not you have obtained a library qualification. Although membership is not cheap, you will find that it is a way of keeping in touch with what is happening in the sector. As a member you will also automatically join a local group, giving you an opportunity to meet other library staff in your vicinity. These contacts may be useful to you and expand your knowledge of the information resources in your locality. In Scotland, the equivalent organisation is CILIPS and in Ireland it is An Chomhairle Leabharlanna.

FIL

A group of staff involved in IDS came together in 1988 to establish a forum for people working in the area or with an interest in it (Forum for

Interlending and Information Delivery – FIL). They had realised that within CILIP there was not a body to deal with the specific needs of IDS staff and that many of them were not, in fact, CILIP members. The Forum was established to address this gap. It was set up as a membership organisation to encourage communication between people working in the field and to provide a means for them to come together to discuss topics of mutual interest.[1] FIL is run by a committee of volunteers drawn from its members and provides a regular Newsletter, an email group, and one-day events and workshops around the country.

FIL conference

FIL also organises an annual conference which runs over three days and is based in a different part of the country on each occasion. The conference fulfils two purposes: first, it gives attendees an excellent opportunity to meet colleagues who are working in the field and allows them to discuss issues in an informal environment; second, there is a programme of speakers and workshops where delegates hear about and discuss issues facing the profession and IDS staff in particular.

Getting involved

If you want to improve the service you offer and learn about what others are doing, FIL is a very useful organisation to join. The relationships that you build with other practitioners will help you in your work. If you need assistance from another institution it is much easier to ask for it when you know the person to whom you are speaking. Although you can attend some FIL events without being a member, it is much better if you are able to join. Members receive a discount on FIL events. You will find information about how to do this on the Forum website.[2] FIL depends upon its members to contribute to its activities: things can only happen when people volunteer. Your own professional development will benefit too, as FIL is a supportive setting in which to learn new skills.

IFLA

IFLA (International Federation of Library Associations and Institutions) is the leading international body representing the interests of library and information services and their users. Founded in Edinburgh in 1927,

IFLA now has over 1700 members in more than 150 countries and has its headquarters in The Hague. IFLA is an independent, international, non-governmental, not-for-profit organisation. Its aims are to promote high standards of provision and delivery of library and information services, encourage widespread understanding of the value of good library and information services, and to represent the interests of its members throughout the world.[3] There are various categories of membership available: institutional membership includes library and information centres, library schools, bibliographic and research institutes, and other institutions or bodies that would like to contribute professionally to the activities of the Federation. If your institution is not already a member, you could recommend that they join. You will then have access to the international world of interlending and the opportunity to network globally with other interlending librarians.

Document Delivery and Resource Sharing Section

Sections are the primary focus for IFLA's work in a particular type of library and information service, in an aspect of library and information science, or in a region, and all IFLA members are entitled to register for Sections of their choice. Sections are grouped into eight Divisions encompassing all aspects of the profession. Division 5, *Collection and Services*, contains seven Sections including *Document Delivery and Resource Sharing*.

The Document Delivery and Resource Sharing Section is the forum for libraries and associations concerned with making information in all formats available throughout the world: its primary objective is to extend and improve document delivery and interlending nationally and internationally through a variety of resource sharing and document supply techniques together with increased co-operation among libraries and document suppliers. To achieve this objective, the Section monitors developments and provides information to its membership through a Section website, twice-yearly newsletter, its *Ask an Expert* service, programmes at IFLA conferences, and co-operative projects with national and international organisations. The Section also oversees the biennial IFLA Interlending & Document Supply International (ILDS) Conference. In addition to these activities, it is responsible for the production and publication of guidelines for international interlending and the IFLA voucher scheme, two important innovations that have facilitated lending between libraries worldwide.

Email group

You may find it useful to subscribe to the lis-ill email group. This is an email discussion group for people working in, or interested in, IDS. Emails sent to the list include practical requests for help or advice and you will often find people asking their colleagues how they are dealing with a particular problem. When new policies or services are introduced there is often a flurry of communication, as practitioners want to find out what everyone else is doing. You will find it a useful way to access the knowledge of those who may be more experienced in IDS than yourself. If you can quote the experience of others it will help you when you need to argue for a particular policy in your own organisation. To subscribe to the group visit the JISCmail Web page.[4] Past debates can be accessed from the list's archive.

Etiquette

Some practitioners also use the list to ask colleagues if they hold more obscure material once they have exhausted all their normal means of sourcing documents. You should be wary, however, of using the list for this purpose too frequently in case you try the patience of your colleagues, and it is worth remembering that some libraries will not respond to a generalised plea for loans or photocopies made in this way.

Journals

If you wish to keep up to date with new ways of working you will find it useful to consult some of the journals in the field.

FIL Newsletter

The *Newsletter* is distributed to all FIL members. As well as reports on FIL business meetings, there are normally articles about recent FIL events or the annual conference. This means that even if you cannot attend meetings you will be able to read something of what was discussed. You will also find reports on new developments of particular relevance to UK and Irish libraries. Because most of the contributions come from other FIL members it is very much shaped by them and their needs.

Interlending and Document Supply

ILDS is the key journal for interlending practitioners in the British Isles. It usually carries detailed and scholarly articles but does sometimes include more practical material. A regular feature in the journal, 'Interlending and document supply: a review of the recent literature'[5] will give you a précis of recent material worldwide. If you do not have easy access to a particular journal, you may consider requesting the articles on inter-library loan!

CILIP Update

Update is distributed to all CILIP members. Many libraries will have a subscription. News items, letters and articles can all be relevant for IDS practitioners.

Further reading

You may wish to find out what developments are taking place outside the UK and Ireland, but you will need to remember that the IDS environment overseas is very different from the UK model. The main North American journal devoted to IDS is the *Journal of InterLibrary Loan, Document Delivery & Electronic Reserve.*[6] Other journals sometimes publish articles of interest to IDS staff, particularly on electronic services.

LISA – Library and Information Science Abstracts

If you do not wish to trawl through all the journals regularly you may find it useful to search on *LISA* for relevant articles. *LISA* is an abstracting service that indexes all the journals relating to librarianship and information science. You may be lucky enough to belong to an institution that subscribes to *LISA* or if you are a CILIP member you can access the service through their website.

Notes

1. For more information about the early days of FIL see: Dean, Elaine and Goodier, Rose (1999) 'Meeting of minds: an account of the history,

development and work of the Forum for Interlending', *Journal of Interlibrary Loan, Document Delivery and Information Supply* 10(2): 31–43.

2. *http://www.cilip.org.uk/fil*
3. See *http://www.ifla.org* for more information about the general work of IFLA.
4. *http://www.jiscmail.ac.uk/lists/lis-ill.html*
5. See, for example: McGrath, Mike (2005) 'Interlending and document supply: a review of recent literature – 51', *Interlending and Document Supply*, 33(1): 42–8.
6. For more information see: *http://www.haworthpress.com/web/JILDD*

Interlending and document supply in different settings

Marian Hesketh and Jenny Brine

Interlending and document supply (IDS) work has many common features irrespective of the sort of library in which it takes place. However, it is worth being aware of the problems encountered in different sectors, as it can make working with them easier.

IDS in public libraries

Public library authorities come in many shapes and sizes, ranging from large counties through metropolitan boroughs and unitary authorities to London boroughs. There is a huge disparity in the size of population within individual authorities, and there are also variations in the way in which they are organised. One distinguishing feature that is peculiar to public libraries is the number of branch and mobile libraries which are served. This means that the end-user can be very remote from the IDS department. Academic, health and special libraries deal with a limited range of requests for material on interlibrary loan, but public libraries deal with requests for absolutely all types. These requests may include those for academic and technical material, but there will also be many requests for books for leisure pursuits, fiction, junior, items in minority languages, talking books for visually impaired borrowers, and music and drama sets.

Statistics for the 10-year period 1991/92–2001/02 show a slight decline in IDS activity in public libraries, from 258,000 items issued in 1991/92 to 252,000 items issued in 2001/02 and from 472,000 items received in 1991/92 to 386,000 items received in 2001/02. This is in line with the general fall in usage of public libraries during this time (Table 6.1).

| Table 6.1 | Public library interlibrary loans 2003–04 (including photocopies issued as substitutes for loans) |

	Within the UK		International		Average time taken to meet borrowers' requests (days)	Percentage of borrowers' requests satisfied
	Issued	Received	Issued	Received		
ENGLAND:						
Inner London	11,519	16,169	41	23	16	85
Outer London	21,969	30,597	49	9	15	87
All London (inc. City)	35,407	48,117	90	32	15	86
Metropolitan Districts	42,161	51,752	69	18	13	93
Unitaries	52,575	80,490	41	97	17	88
Counties	103,043	134,024	324	1062	18	92
TOTAL ENGLAND	233,186	314,383	524	1209	17	91
WALES	5712	14,357	20	7	12	90
ENGLAND & WALES	238,898	328,740	544	1216	16	91
SCOTLAND	7951	16,078	32	23	15	90
NORTHERN IRELAND	620	2437	132	169	8	76
UNITED KINGDOM	247,469	347,255	708	1408	16	90

Source: LISU Public Library Statistics 2003–2004, Table N

The organisation of IDS in a public library setting is different in many ways from that found in academic libraries in that it would be rare to find a separate department called 'Inter Library Loans'; IDS is usually part of a general Requests or Bibliographical Services department, and books are often bought to satisfy requests. Public libraries are much less likely than academic libraries to use a stand-alone ILL package to organise their requests. For example, ILLOS is one of the most popular ILL packages, but of the 43 libraries which were using it in January 2005, only four were public library authorities. Five other public libraries had been users in the past but had stopped using it; most transferred to the ILL module within their local Library Management System. Other options for organising ILL within public libraries are to use the management system within LinkUK (formerly Viscount), the UnityWeb messaging system or a paper-based system.

A look at the published statistics for IDS in public libraries will soon identify the huge variations and disparities between different types of public library authorities. The largest county library systems will lend and borrow several thousand items each year whereas the smallest authorities deal with fewer than 100 items. The average proportion of IDS requests which are satisfied over the whole of the UK is 88%, but the figures reported by individual authorities range from 99% to 39%. Similarly, the average speed of supply for IDS in public libraries over the whole country is 18 days, but individual authorities report an average ranging from a leisurely 39 days to a very speedy 3 days. It would be possible to conclude from this that some of the statistics supplied are more accurate than others, and also that access to IDS via public libraries is not uniform across the country, with some library authorities giving a better service than others.

Public Library Standards were first published in 2001, and a revised list was issued in 2004.[1] The purpose of the standards is to set up a performance monitoring framework for public libraries, and the standard which has most relevance for IDS is PLSS5, which sets targets for speed of supply of requested books. Fifty per cent should be supplied within 7 days, 70% within 15 days and 85% within 30 days, counting from the time the reservation is made until the time when the borrower is informed that the book is available. However, the vast majority of requests made are for items already in the library's stock, or on order; only a very small proportion of requests are for IDS material, and the Public Library Standards have had little or no impact on IDS in public libraries. IDS is not regarded as a top-level indicator of performance and is not seen as an important part of the service when it comes to influencing policy-makers.

Many public libraries, but by no means all, charge more for IDS than they do for requests for material already held in their own stock. In some cases, the charge is deliberately set at a high level to discourage demand which could not be satisfied; for example, Edinburgh City Libraries charge £5.00 for an IDS request to discourage use of the service by students who could use their college or university library instead, but this may also discourage use by members of the public who have no alternative source of supply. In small authorities, staffing can be a problem in addition to the lack of financial resources. Sometimes only one member of staff deals with IDS and there is no cover for absences. Some IDS staff report a feeling of being undervalued and that their work appears to be of little interest to senior management.

Given that small authorities appear to be struggling to provide an efficient IDS service on their own, it is no surprise that there is a growing trend towards co-operation. In Wales, three small authorities (Gwynedd, Ynys Môn and Conwy) have combined to operate as a single unit. A consortium in London called 'Open Galaxy' links the boroughs of Havering, Redbridge and Wandsworth, and the quick and easy inter-loan of materials between participating libraries is one of its major benefits.[2] An ambitious project and pointer for the future is found in the South West region of England.[3] 'Wisdom' is an initiative which allows users of participating libraries to search the catalogues of several other libraries in the region simultaneously. Reservations can be made online, and the book will be sent to the user's chosen library and the fee charged when the book is collected.

The government report 'Framework for the Future'[4] has a vision for libraries in 2013 which includes a comprehensive IDS service:

> Anyone seeking a book can be guaranteed to get access to it through the library whether or not it is still in print.

A recent report by the Laser Foundation[5] envisages a more flexible approach to the delivery of material, with the possibility of premium delivery to the borrower's home for an extra fee. Both of these reports present huge challenges to the public library IDS community. Customers are also becoming more demanding and expectations of service have been fuelled by online services such as Amazon. The future for IDS in public libraries undoubtedly includes much more co-operation and an expansion of services to meet these new demands.

Case study – Lancashire County Library

Lancashire is one of the largest county councils, serving a population of approximately 1.1 million, and the library service has more than 80 service points. IDS is part of the Requests section within the centralised Bibliographical Services department in Preston. As in most public library authorities, IDS is only part of the work of the section and almost all staff do other work in addition to IDS. An electronic template, designed in-house, is used to transmit requests quickly to the Requests section. Initial bibliographical checking is done on UnityWeb and LinkUK, and other databases used include Talisbase and COPAC. Lancashire is one of the few public library authorities which uses the ILLOS IDS package to manage their loans. ILLOS has been used in Lancashire since 1990, and is an excellent and comprehensive tool. Total IDS applications in 2004/05 were 13,911, and a paper-based system could not possibly cope with this level of activity. In 2004/05, 13,350 items were received, a success rate of 96%, with an average supply time of 12.9 days.

Any type of material which is available for IDS can be requested, and there is a standard charge of 60p per request, with no distinction being made between items supplied on IDS and those supplied from the library's own stock. Photocopies account for 11.2% of the total receipts. Fiction accounts for 6.86% of all requests and 7.72% of book requests. Almost half of all receipts (42%) come from the British Library (BL), with the rest spread fairly evenly between the North West region and the rest of the country. Only a handful of international loans are received each year. Most of the items not supplied by the BL come from other public libraries; 44.8% of all receipted loans come from public libraries and only 12.02% from academic libraries. This reflects the type of material requested and the fact that most higher level material comes from the BL.

Like most public libraries, Lancashire is a net borrower. In 2004/05, 14,311 IDS requests to borrow were received, of which 9976 were supplied. Many outgoing loans can be supplied from the extensive reserve stock at county library headquarters; holds are placed on the Talis library management system for items held at branch libraries. On arrival at headquarters, they are issued and packed for dispatch. All IDS loans are recorded and managed on the Talis system.

Lancashire County Library has a large, well-funded IDS operation which is one of the biggest players in the market.

Case study – East Lothian libraries

East Lothian council is a small authority to the east of Edinburgh, serving a predominantly rural community. The population is approximately 90,000. At present there are no further or higher education institutions within the authority, although a university campus is due to open in 2007. The library service has 12 branches and two mobile libraries. With a total budget for IDS of £5000 per year, some restrictions have to be made. IDS requests are not normally made for students, other than distance- or open-learning students, and junior items are not borrowed except for schools. Fiction is not normally borrowed, and books about leisure topics such as craft, gardening and cookery are only occasionally requested. Request charges are 35p for a self-reservation of an in-stock item, 45p for a reservation made in the library and £1.00 for an IDS item. Individual borrowers are limited to 25 IDS requests per year; few come near this limit, but a charge of £5.00 per IDS item would be made for additional requests.

Budget restrictions mean that East Lothian libraries do not subscribe to any databases. The Talis IDS module is used to make and manage requests, and Talisbase, CAIRNS and COPAC are used for location searching. Local Scottish resources are heavily used, and the National Library of Scotland can provide locations from the Scottish union catalogue and LinkUK. SESLIN (South East Scotland Learning Information Network) is a local scheme which allows East Lothian libraries to borrow books from Napier University outside the normal IDS channels. In 2003/04, 80 items were obtained in this way.

In 2003/04, East Lothian libraries received 1175 IDS items for customers in libraries and 41 for schools. The majority came from other libraries in Scotland, with only 54 being received from the BL. Only 235 items were lent out. East Lothian is an example of a very small authority working within budget restrictions to provide the best possible service.[6]

Case study – Westminster libraries

Westminster is an inner London borough serving a very diverse population, including many commuters and visitors. Like many local authorities, it has been subjected to a number of reorganisations and restructurings, and these have affected the IDS service, which has been decentralised and re-centralised more than once. Branch library staff struggled to deal with IDS work on top of their frontline commitments, resulting in backlogs of work and the payment of large penalties for the non-return of loans. The IDS service is now centralised, with 2½ full-time equivalent staff, and the supply time of IDS items has been halved.

The primary IDS tool is LinkUK (formerly Viscount), which is used for bibliographical checking and requesting. Staff at Westminster find the LinkUK system quick and responsive. The takeover of LinkUK by OCLC is seen as a good thing, bringing in more funding and expertise and leading towards the possibility of searching LinkUK and Worldcat together. COPAC and Worldcat are also used for location checking, but the extra expense of a subscription to UnityWeb cannot be justified. There is also an in-house reservations database called REDAM, which tracks IDS loans through the system and can be accessed by staff in branch libraries. Loans are added to the GEAC library management system, and deleted when the book is returned. In many public library systems, the IDS end-user is remote from the centralised IDS department, and branch library staff do not always have access to IDS systems to answer enquiries about renewals etc. Westminster libraries' IDS staff try to bypass the branch libraries and build a personal relationship with their end-users; one way of doing this is to include the direct telephone number of the IDS department on the date labels of IDS material.

In 2003/04, Westminster libraries made 3764 IDS applications, of which 3078 were supplied, a success rate of 82%. The vast majority (2355) were supplied from other libraries within the London region, with 551 coming from the British Library Document Supply Centre (BLDSC) and only 150 from the rest of the UK. Westminster makes more applications abroad than most other public library authorities, using the requesting facilities of Worldcat; 40 applications to foreign libraries were made in 2003/04, and 22 of these were successful. Customer focus is very important to Westminster's IDS staff, and many of their users are non-residents who use their service because they find it better than the other options open to them.[7]

IDS in libraries in education

Education libraries encompass a wide range of services, from learning resource centres in schools and further education colleges through enormous collections in universities to the great copyright libraries in Oxford and Cambridge. Their involvement with IDS also varies. Some do no IDS work at all, whereas the heaviest users of the service send out nearly 33,000 requests a year. In 2002/03 higher and further education institutions alone received nearly 1 million items, and they supplied nearly 180,000 items to other libraries.[8]

Universities

University libraries have a number of factors in common in their provision of IDS, but there are considerable differences in how they fund and deliver the service. Universities are undergoing enormous changes, which affect all parts of the library service, including IDS. The increase in the numbers of undergraduates has had a limited effect on IDS, as most institutions provide materials required for teaching from their own stock. However, expansions in postgraduate courses have increased the demand for research materials. This has coincided with the rapid growth of online databases and the Internet, which have made researchers more aware of the enormous range of information available on their subject. At the same time, universities have been able to expand greatly the range of titles offered to readers because of the explosion in the provision of e-journals. The latest summary of trends notes:

> Inter-library lending has fallen again this year, and is now at less than half the level of ten years ago. The factors behind this are likely to be complex, and may include the imposition of departmental quotas intended to keep costs low, the ease with which users can bypass the library to purchase direct from commercial document delivery suppliers, and the increasing availability of journal titles now available electronically in every library.[9]

Interlending of books, rather than the provision of copies of articles, is likely to become a greater proportion of the work of the IDS department. However, at present most universities receive more articles than books. It remains to be seen whether e-books can supplant real books in the way that online journals are replacing print subscriptions.

University libraries generally enjoy a high level of computer provision and IT support compared with other public-sector institutions. Many computer-based experiments in IDS services, such as EDDIS and EASY, originated in universities. Fax machines and emails have been commonplace for far longer than in public or health libraries. All are members of JISC and so benefit from subscriptions to a large range of sophisticated databases and datasets. These include the ZETOC service from the BL (known as Inside to commercial users), the range of databases available through Edinburgh University (EDINA) and those from the Online Computer Library Center, Inc. (OCLC) such as Worldcat. In addition, universities subscribe to a wide range of indexes and abstracting services which support their own particular fields of interest.

Universities, almost without exception, use computer-based IDS management systems, often sophisticated packages provided by their Library Management System (LMS), or stand-alone packages such as ILLOS.

Policies vary widely on charging for the IDS service. In some libraries, readers have to buy a request form for a small sum, whereas others charge an amount much closer to the BL's prices. In some institutions, the cost of IDS is charged to departments, which assume responsibility for rationing use if necessary. Yet others make no charge to individuals, but top-slice a department's library allocations to fund the IDS service. Like other UK public-sector institutions, universities benefit from a discount from the BL on its document supply services.

The internal organisation of IDS varies enormously. Some institutions do a great deal of bibliographical checking and location work in-house, whereas others rely on the services of the BL or a regional organisation. Some are heavily involved in their regional library networks and work with local public libraries, and others deal almost exclusively with the BL and other universities. Some universities are investigating unmediated requesting services. Most universities will get material from abroad for their readers, whether through the BL's World Wide Search service, through groups such as RLN or OCLC, or direct.

Universities require a very wide range of material through IDS, ranging from foreign-language literary texts through conference papers on engineering, patents and standards, to popular non-fiction. Many also lend and borrow music. In the sector as a whole, success rates for IDS applications are around 94%. Statistical data on libraries in higher and further education are now collected by SCONUL. Member institutions can access statistical data online.

The need for interlibrary loan in many universities is being reduced by reciprocal borrowing schemes such as SCONUL Research Extra and UK Libraries Plus. They enable users to travel to the libraries which hold the books, rather than needing the book to come to the reader's home library.[10]

Case study: Leeds University Library

Leeds University Library is one of the largest libraries in the UK. Its holdings are well known to the academic community in Britain and abroad through its records on COPAC and its involvement in SHARES. The library is on several sites – the Brotherton Library collects humanities and social sciences; the Edward Boyle Library holds sciences and engineering and houses the Student Library (a collection of core texts for undergraduates covering all subjects); medicine and health literature is in the Health Sciences Library and St James University Hospital Library; Bretton Hall holds material on performance arts and the cultural industries; and Wakefield provides resources for part-time students undertaking Continuing Education courses. All IDS requests from Leeds readers and external libraries are processed at the Brotherton Library using the ILLOS management system. Requests may be submitted online or using paper forms, and Secure Electronic Delivery (SED) is available. A flat rate charge of £2 is made for each request, and this applies to both staff and students. Some departments may refund the costs to their researchers. Leeds has pioneered an unmediated document delivery service, 'Documents Direct', based on the BL's Inside Web service;[11] this is funded by 'top-slicing' departmental library allocations. Another special factor affecting Leeds is its proximity to the BL: day visits to the Reading Room at Boston Spa are perfectly practical, and a minibus service for students and staff of Leeds, and Leeds Metropolitan University, makes a regular weekly trip. Leeds requested 14,074 items in 2004/05, with a 93% success rate. Leeds is a valued source of loans for the rest of the library community, and lent 9200 items the same year. Leeds is not a member of Conarls.[12]

Case study: Lancaster University Library

Lancaster University Library (LUL) is a medium-sized institution serving around 10,000 undergraduates and around 2000 postgraduates. In 2004/05 readers submitted 12,086 requests, of which 10,146 resulted in applications and 9554 were received (94% success rate). A significant percentage of reader requests are for material which turns out to be available in the library, either in hard copy or electronically. Unlike for most universities, the number of requests to IDS has not fallen much in recent years, mainly because of a policy decision to service a large new course in Clinical Psychology via IDS rather than purchases.

LUL uses the ILLOS IDS management system and encourages users to apply online and receive documents through SED.

LUL carries out detailed bibliographical checking on all book requests, both to save time and to avoid the BL's search charges. Where possible, books are borrowed from other libraries within the North West to keep costs down. LUL is not a Conarls member, so if books are not available in the North West the next application is made to the BL. After that, a wide range of university and public libraries are used. Requests for journal articles in the health field are sent to LIHNN libraries (see below), but otherwise all journal articles are passed to the BL unverified. The library did not take part in the serials co-operative LAMDA. Detailed checking is carried out on serials requests only if they fail at the BL or appear suspicious. LUL receives material from abroad via the BL's World Wide Search service, or by dealing direct with foreign libraries, as it is not a member of RLN or OCLC. Eighty-five per cent of the journal articles received come from the BL, but only 51% of books. The importance of library networks is demonstrated by the fact that LUL receives material from around 230 different institutions in the UK and abroad each year.

As an active member of UnityWeb, LUL lends to libraries within the North West for the cost of transport, and to other libraries throughout the UK. In 2004/05 they lent 3074 items. In an average month, LUL provides material to about 90 other libraries. IDS forms part of the Services section of the library and all staff take part in regular timetabled duties on the issue and enquiry desks.

Case study: Cambridge University Library

Cambridge University Library (CUL) houses one of the largest and oldest collections in the UK, and lies at the heart of a complex system of college and departmental libraries. (A number of these collections stand aloof from the IDS system.) It has important collections of foreign-language materials. The library benefits from Legal Deposit and has large amounts of older British publications not listed in its online catalogues. Its holdings are reported to COPAC very regularly, and its periodicals holdings form part of SUNCAT.

Unlike the other legal deposit libraries, CUL has always been a lending library. It was therefore very willing to become a 'back-up' library to the BL in 1974. By the 1980s, CUL was the principal back-up library, supplying around 30,000 items a year. This service was always required to be self-financing. When the 'back-up' system ended in 2001, Cambridge decided to try to continue the service, still covering all of its costs, including staff, photocopying and postage. CUL charges other libraries slightly more than normal UK rates, and lends books for library use only, but is greatly valued by the library community for its willingness to share its collections. Some of the other libraries within Cambridge University act as 'back-ups' to CUL, but others are now independent. CUL receives requests from all parts of the UK and Ireland; requests from libraries abroad do not come direct but are sent from the BL. It supplies far more loans and photocopies than it receives – in 2002/03 it supplied 12,519 items, compared with 5782 requests made by its readers.

Cambridge University members are charged £3 per request, non-members £6. ILLOS is used to process outgoing requests. However, a third of other libraries within Cambridge University process requests for their members, and some do not charge at all. This reduces the number of requests handled by CUL.[13]

Colleges

Colleges of further (FE) and higher education (HE) use IDS to supplement the teaching and research materials in their own stocks. In most cases this will be limited to staff, and students undertaking project work. Some rely on paper systems, whereas others use the interlending package provided by their LMS. IDS provision – like other library and information services – is often complicated by having to serve a large number of small sites. The level of institutional IT support is uneven. The sector has access to a number of databases and e-journal collections, but not to the full range of JISC services. Many FE colleges have close links with a university in their region, and have preferential access to that collection. Local co-operative schemes, such as ALLISS in Lancashire, make it easier for students and staff at FE and HE colleges to access local university libraries. However, IDS is still important. Institutions of this size tend to make heavy use of local networks to keep borrowing costs down, and to borrow far more than they lend.

Schools

Few school libraries make much use of the IDS system; where additional material is required, teachers will turn to the local public library for help, deal with the BL direct on the basis of a credit-card transaction or perhaps ask a favour of a local university.

Libraries in government, industry and commerce

Libraries in government, industry and commerce focus on the work of their parent organisation, and serve a restricted circle of users. The number of library and information services in the sector has declined over the last 20 years, and many existing services have contracted in response to the increased availability of documents electronically.[14] Some have to serve staff across the globe – for instance, the GlaxoSmithKline (GSK) document delivery team provides books and articles to users in the USA, Italy, Spain, France and Japan, as well as the UK.[15] IDS services in this sector are often prepared to pay a higher price in return for fast and efficient service. In 2003, GSK provided 95% of documents requested within 5 days, and 80% within 2 days.

Many special libraries subscribe to a large number of specialist journals in their areas, both in print form and as e-journals, and are very willing to buy additional materials as downloads. Some maintain large archives of report literature and have significant holdings of older journals; others focus on current literature. Many will purchase material in response to requests, turning to IDS as an exception.

Libraries in industry and commerce around the world are important customers of the BL, accounting for nearly a third of the items it supplies.[16] They pay the full BL price for a photocopy, plus a copyright fee to the journal publisher. They pioneered the BL's Secure Electronic Delivery Service, and small- and medium-sized firms are expected to be heavy users of British Library Direct. This sector has always explored a wide range of commercial document delivery services alongside – or instead of – the BL.[17] UK government libraries benefit from the same discount on BL services as other public-sector institutions.

When borrowing books, special libraries make much less use of co-operative networks than public sector libraries do. However, some are members of regional organisations such as Libraries North West (LNW) or LIEM, largely for training and information. Nearly all pay the BL to provide locations for books and journals which it does not hold itself.

Case study – BAe Systems Warton

Warton is one of several sites which make up BAe Systems. In the past, some of these other sites belonged to different companies and this has resulted in a number of historical differences and incompatibilities between the sites. Library staff from all the sites meet each other, and would like to improve standardisation between libraries, but at present the company has other priorities. Some IDS takes place between sites, particularly between Warton, Brough and Farnborough, which have a common catalogue.

IDS items received at Warton consist of 70% books and 30% journal articles. Almost all of the journals relevant to the site's primary business of military aircraft production are purchased, either in hard copy or electronically. Items requested on IDS tend to be for peripheral subjects such as management and airfield support, medical topics or air traffic control. Report literature is also important in this research environment, but again most of what is needed is available internally. The BLDSC is the main source for IDS, but the library staff will also check COPAC and try other libraries if BLDSC cannot supply. In a commercial library such as this, paying the full BLDSC rate, IDS is expensive and costs must be controlled. There is no charge to the user for IDS, as the material is needed for work purposes, but if an IDS application appeared to be leading towards a substantial cost, the user would be contacted and asked if it were really essential. Library staff report that some users feel that because they need the information for their work, this gives them the right to keep IDS loans for as long as possible. The Library and Information Services team at BAe Systems Warton serve a clientele with specialised and highly focused needs. Most of the material required can be supplied from stock, but IDS plays an important role in complementing the library's own resources and supporting the work of the company.[18]

Case study: British Geological Survey

The British Geological Survey (BGS) is responsible for advising the UK government on all aspects of geoscience as well as providing impartial geological advice to industry, academia and the public. It is part of the Natural Environment Research Council (NERC). The BGS has a number of sites in the UK, and also has staff based on overseas projects. There are libraries at the two main UK sites, Keyworth near Nottingham, and Edinburgh. At Wallingford, Oxfordshire, where the BGS shares a site with the Centre for Ecology and Hydrology (CEH), a collection is held within the CEH Library premises.

The library was founded in the 1840s and contains a substantial collection on the earth sciences, including books, journals, maps, photographs and archival material. Provision of electronic resources such as e-journals is increasingly important. Libraries at the Keyworth and Edinburgh sites are open to the public, for reference, and a visitor photocopying service is available. There are co-operative IDS arrangements with other NERC libraries. Loans are available to BGS staff and NERC staff, but IDS services to other libraries are limited to the provision of photocopies. IDS services to BGS staff from Keyworth totalled 885 requests in 2004/05, and over a quarter of these were satisfied by documents from within BGS or from other NERC libraries. Nearly all other requests were supplied from the BL. In 2004/05 Edinburgh handled 287 requests, with about half being satisfied by Keyworth Library. The library at Keyworth has noted a decrease in the number of requests to the BL over the last 2 years, which may be due to increased checking of requests and the increased availability of e-journals. The library uses a simple multipart request form to manage IDS requests. They are all verified. The aim is to check all requests within 1 working day, and if an external loan is required, to send requests to the BL within 3 working days (requests are often sent sooner than this). From Keyworth requests are sent to BL using ARTTel; Edinburgh uses ArtWeb. If requests have to be sourced elsewhere, this is usually done directly by telephone or email. The library is considering offering SED to its users, and is also looking at automating IDS procedures using the VDX module with OLIB, its library management software. It is interested in using electronic signatures for requests if this becomes legally permissible.[19]

Health libraries

Health libraries are a large and diverse group. There are large, long-established university libraries attached to teaching hospitals, such as the Barnes Medical Library in Birmingham. Some hospitals have had libraries for many years, serving GPs and hospital doctors. Alongside these well-established collections, there has been a rapid growth in recent years of smaller collections supporting primary care trusts (PCTs). Existing health libraries have also been undergoing considerable reorganisation. Many nursing and medical libraries have merged to create multidisciplinary libraries serving all health professionals. At one time many health libraries were run by unqualified staff, but over the last two decades the drive towards evidence-based medicine has made a high-quality professionally run service increasingly important. However, there are many small units, often open part-time. Some GPs have their own collections, and supplement this by using their local hospitals, public library or PCT.

The IDS arrangements for these libraries vary considerably. Many of the large collections have had BL accounts for many years, and play a full part in the national interlending scene. The collections of Birmingham, Leeds, Nottingham, Newcastle and others appear on COPAC along with that of the university library of which they are a part. Many health libraries are heavy users of the services of the BL.

However, most health libraries use a variety of document sources. In many cases, a major incentive to avoid the BL is cost. Members of many co-operatives send photocopies to each other free of charge. At a national level, an important source of 'free' copies is the *Nursing Union List of Journals*, which has existed since 1987. Some libraries are members of the Psychiatric Libraries Co-operative Scheme. Regional co-operation is also vital. For example, in the North West of England, the Library Information Health Network Northwest (LIHNN) compiles a union catalogue of serials in medicine, nursing and professions allied to medicine, and members supply copies of journal articles to each other free of charge. Many health libraries are linked to local medical schools or other providers of health education, and can obtain copies of articles from them at preferential rates. At a national level, a number of organisations provide library services to their members. Many health libraries are members of professional organisations such as the British Medical Association (BMA) or the Royal College of Surgeons. Both supply photocopies far more cheaply than the BL does. As the price varies radically according to where an article comes from, readers are often asked in advance to state how much they are prepared to pay for an article. Sometimes costs are recharged to departments or research budgets, whereas in others the individual pays cash.

Health libraries have a variety of library management systems, and some use the ILL packages provided. Many use the WINchILL software, which was designed for health libraries by librarians at the Christie Hospital in Manchester. However, many use simple paper-based systems. Whereas some libraries rely on photocopies, others make heavy use of SED.

Health professionals out in the community often make use of their local public library, or the library of their professional organisation, rather than health service libraries.

The sort of material health libraries request through IDS is very varied. To give examples of the sort of material health libraries request:

- A surgeon asks for an article to be faxed through because it has diagrams needed for an operation planned for the following day. A neighbouring Trust holds the journal and sends the article in response to a phone call.

- A nurse on a medium-secure psychiatric unit needs information on managing a new patient. The librarian's literature search throws up a number of interesting articles, most of which are not available in the small collection on-site. Request forms are sent out by fax to libraries at other units in the North West within a few days.

- A consultant is revising procedures and wants review articles on a particular illness. The union list locates some of the journals locally, but three are ordered from the BMA and one from the BL.

- A public health worker is preparing for a campaign on smoking. The librarian borrows several books from other local libraries, and gets report literature from another PCT.

- A junior doctor is preparing for exams and asks the library to borrow copies of textbooks and Q&A books. As they are in demand elsewhere in the region, she is advised to buy her own copies.

Statistical information about health libraries is the responsibility of the National Health Service Library and Knowledge Development Network (LKDN). All health libraries are asked to complete annual returns, which are collated and analysed by the Library and Information Statistics Unit at Loughborough University (LISU). Activity data collected include interlibrary loans and the supply and receipt of journal articles within the local network of health libraries, from the BL, and from other sources such as the BMA.[20]

Libraries in different parts of the UK and Ireland

The principles of IDS are broadly similar throughout the UK and Ireland. However, the local regional library service can make a considerable difference to how IDS is practised. There is more information about regional organisations in Chapter 4.

For historical reasons the Irish library service is built on the same model as that of the UK. Library co-operation between Northern Ireland and the Republic of Ireland is facilitated by The Committee on Library Co-operation in Ireland (COLICO), which also acts in an advisory capacity to An Chomhairle Leabharlanna (Library Council) and to the Library and Information Services Council (LISC) Northern Ireland. IDS is part of COLICO'S remit, and it liaises with the BL and also collects and publishes annual interlending statistics for libraries in Northern Ireland and the Republic of Ireland.

Irish libraries, both north and south, are heavily dependent on the services of the BL. Libraries in the Republic of Ireland are obviously not entitled to the concessionary prices granted to the UK public-sector organisations, and are charged at UK domestic commercial rates. Nevertheless, Irish libraries from north and south take part in the UK interlending network, and are included in the BL Directory of Codes and may be debited and credited through the BL banker function, although charges made by Irish libraries may vary. Trinity College Dublin maintains its Copyright Library status, and is a useful and good source for British material. It is the only Irish member of the Consortium for Research Libraries (CURL) and its holdings are included on COPAC. None of the Northern Ireland university library holdings is included on COPAC. IRIS, the consortium of Irish University and Research Libraries, is developing a union catalogue of its members' holdings. Ireland is represented on Conarls by An Chomhairle Leabharlanna, which also manages the bibliographic update of Irish libraries for inclusion in UnityWeb. Irish libraries do not use transport systems for the return of loanable items.[21]

Scottish libraries benefit from a close relationship with the National Library of Scotland, which provides a free-of-charge locations service. There are several thriving regional co-operation schemes within Scotland. Scottish libraries also lend to each other at a reduced rate (SILLR). Nationally many are members of the Conarls scheme, which also allows reduced cost loans. Many public and university libraries report their holdings to UnityWeb. The CAIRNS service facilitates resource sharing within Scotland, although at present response times from OPAC searches are slow. Edinburgh, Aberdeen and Glasgow universities report their holdings to COPAC, and the machine-readable part of the catalogue of the National Library of Scotland is also there.

Libraries in Wales have no regional organisation at present (see Chapter 5), but a number of local groups are partially filling the gap. Some public and university libraries report their holdings to UnityWeb, others to LinkUK. The holdings of the National Library of Wales are on COPAC, as are the Special Collections at Lampeter, but at present no other Welsh universities are listed there.

In England, the regional library organisations vary widely in their activities. This has a marked effect on IDS work, particularly in public libraries. Those in London and the South East, and the West Midlands, focus on LinkUK; the others have UnityWeb as their main focus for co-operation. Nevertheless, the BL acts as the lynchpin of the system for all the regions.

Appendix: websites

LISU

http://www.lboro.ac.uk/departments/dils/lisu/index.html

SCONUL

http://www.sconul.ac.uk/

Nursing Union List of Journals

http://wads.le.ac.uk/li/clinical/nulj_homepage.htm

LIHNN

http://www.aditus.nhs.uk/Aditus/Communities/Librarians+LIHNN/default.htm

Notes

1. Lightfoot, David (2004) 'Changing forms, changing futures', *Public Library Journal* Winter: 8–10.
2. Francis, Vivienne (2005) 'Open galaxy', *Public Library Journal* Spring: 12–14.
3. *http://www.wisdom-sw.net*
4. DCMS (2003) *Framework for the Future*, p. 51. Available online at: *http://www.culture.gov.uk/global/publications/archive_2003/framework_future.htm*
5. Laser Foundation (2005) *Libraries: a Vision. The Public Library Service in 2015.* Available online at: *http://www.futuresgroup.org.uk/index.php?pageid=5&docid=23*
6. We are grateful to the staff of East Lothian libraries for allowing us to visit them and collect information about their service.
7. We are grateful to Kofi Mensah for arranging a visit to Westminster libraries for us and providing us with information about their service.
8. LISU (2004) *SCONUL Annual Library Statistics 2002–03.* Loughborough University: LISU.
9. Creaser, Clare (2005) *SCONUL Library statistics: trend analysis to 2003–2004.* Loughborough University: LISU, p. 2
10. Goodier, Rose and Dean, Elaine (2004) 'Changing patterns in interlibrary loans and document supply', *Interlending and Document Supply* 32(4): 206–14.

11. Birch, K. and Young, I.A. (2001) 'Unmediated document delivery at Leeds: from project to operational system', *Interlending and Document Supply* 29(1): 4–10. [This service may not continue after 2006; Birch and Young, personal communication.]

12. We are grateful to Wendy Calvert of Leeds University Library for checking this section.

13. We are grateful to Barry Eaden of Cambridge University Library for providing information for this case study.

14. For an example of a slimmed down library and document supply service, see: Broadshaw, Sheila (1997) 'Outsourcing document supply – the BT experience', *Interlending and Document Supply* 25(3): 108–12.

15. Delaney, Emma L. (2003) 'GlaxoSmithKline Pharmaceuticals research and development: document delivery in a global corporate environment', *Interlending and Document Supply* 31(1): 15–20.

16. In 2000/01, 31%, according to the figures in: British Library (2001) *British Library 28th Annual Report and Accounts, 2000-2001*. London: British Library.

17. There is a useful explanation of the suppliers used at the Merck, Sharpe and Dohme Neuroscience Research Centre in: Chambers, Janice (1999) 'End-user document supply or who needs an interlibrary loans service? A special library's perspective', *Interlending and Document Supply* 27(2): 71–9.

18. We are most grateful to BAe for allowing us to visit their library and information service.

19. We are most grateful to Joan Bird of the BGS for providing this information.

20. We are grateful to members of LIHNN who arranged library visits for us and to David Stewart of the North West Health Care Libraries Unit for checking this section.

21. We are grateful to Avril Patterson of University College Dublin for the section on IDS in Ireland.

7

Interlending and document supply: different sorts of materials

Jenny Brine

Staff in interlending and document supply (IDS) deal with a wide variety of materials. In many cases, we need to verify the information before we send it to another library or to the British Library (BL). We may also need to find out which library holds the item, so we can decide which institution to approach first. Libraries vary considerably in their policy on checking before applying to the BL. A study in 1995 showed that some bibliographical checking in the originating library does help ensure the request is ultimately successful.[1] Since then, the BL has introduced charges for providing locations and many more libraries now do some location work themselves. In certain regions, such as the North West, the regional library service provides a bibliographical checking and location service. The provision of bibliographical databases and union catalogues over the Web, whether for a subscription or free of charge, has made it much easier for libraries to undertake their own verification and location work. The amount of checking and location work a library will do depends on (a) local policies, (b) staff time and (c) the databases to which it has access.

This chapter aims to explain why certain sorts of material pose particular difficulties for IDS staff and indicate strategies for solving the problems. Although the detail may change quite rapidly as new services become available and others cease, the general principles should remain the same. Websites mentioned in the course of the chapter are listed in the Appendix.

Where do readers get their information from? And why do mistakes happen?

Readers seldom invent book or journal titles. The most likely sources of requests are as follows.

References in another book or journal

Readers often want to follow up ideas or facts in a book or article they have read. Despite electronic databases, following other researchers' citations is a popular way of building a bibliography. Most references will be adequate. However, possible problems include:

- The author may have made a mistake. Subeditors do sometimes verify references in the books or journals for which they are responsible, but this is not always the case. Writers sometimes quote a source document without actually seeing it for themselves. They may rely on an earlier citation, which was incorrect. It may be very difficult to get back to the correct source for a statement. It can also be very hard to convince readers that their source of reference is wrong.

- In older books in particular, the references may be correct but the details very skimpy. It can take someone with a good knowledge of 19th century British journals to work out the abbreviations.

- The reader may get muddled. The most common problems are: requesting a journal article by author and title as if it were a book; requesting a chapter in a book produced under editorial direction as if it were a book; not understanding the abbreviations the author has used, which may have been spelt out at the beginning of the bibliography or in a preface; not understanding conventional scholarly abbreviations (such as *loc. cit.*).

- The reader may not realise that if a book or article is 'in press' or 'in preparation' or 'forthcoming' it may not have been published, or may have appeared in another form in a completely different publication. Sometimes a reader may not understand the nature of scientific communication and want to follow up a piece of information referenced as 'personal communication'.[2]

- Newspapers and popular magazines often refer to books and articles, but give little bibliographical information. Book reviews may have a title for the review that is rather different to that of the book or books under review. The reader may give the review title instead of the book title. The weekly *Books in the media* can help; in mid-2005, however, this was absorbed by *The Bookseller*. Obituaries often make mention of a person's written works but without giving sufficient information.[3] Sports magazines are notorious for referring to recent medical literature without giving a full reference.

Oral information

This includes articles or books mentioned in lectures and tutorials, on the radio or TV, or in conversation. The difficulty here is that the speaker may be giving out information in an impromptu way. Our reader is then working from memory, which is often inexact. Furthermore, in English the spoken word is often not good at transmitting correct spellings, particularly of names. The user may give us the spelling of a name they believe they heard, such as Davis for Davies or Perry instead of Perrie. They may also write down the sense of the book title, rather than its exact wording.

Databases

As more databases are now available online, readers are willing to use them rather than plough through paper indexes to the literature. This does make a far wider range of literature available to our readers and encourages them to look beyond the confines of their own library. The problems which can arise include:

- The reader does not understand how to extract the salient details from the citation. Many databases give so much information that the essentials are not obvious. So you may find the reader quoting the name of the institution which produces a journal rather than the title of the journal itself. First names and surnames can be inverted, or so much space on the request form taken up listing all the authors in full that the reader has no space left for the title of the article.

- The database may cover material in a number of different languages. If the journal title is presented in English translation as well as in the original language, the reader may quote that alone. Users may not realise that the article is in a foreign language and be surprised to receive an article in a language they do not understand, with perhaps just an abstract in English.

- The database may cover publications which are not widely held in the UK. The MLA Bibliography, for instance, covers many US college journals which are produced in small quantities and may only be preserved in the library of that particular college plus the Library of Congress.
- There may be an error in the database.

The Internet

The Internet covers a huge range of sources, of course. The main points to note are:

- Many readers quote bibliographical data from Amazon or similar sites without appreciating that the books listed may not be available in the UK, may be out of print or may not yet have been published.
- Data on the internet have often not gone through any editing process and so mistakes are not corrected.
- The Web can give access to documents intended for internal use within organisations, such as reading lists or working papers, or even students' essays. Material may be in a preliminary form, or merely circulated for discussion.
- Bibliographies on the Web, particularly those created by fans of a particular author or musician or artist, may be created in a spirit of enthusiasm rather than accuracy. They may also draw on alternative press materials which are not widely held.
- Academics and researchers often list their works on their own homepage. These are not always accurate. Furthermore, they often list unpublished reports and papers. Sometimes an email to the author may elicit the correct information or even an offer to send the paper required.
- A reader may have found an article in a mainstream journal via a Web search, but could not access the full text of the article because the institution does not subscribe to it. In some cases it may turn out that the library subscribes to the journal in paper form, but the reader has not checked. It is worth noting that if the article is not available from a library in the UK, it can be cheaper to pay for a download than apply abroad.

Copying errors

Many mistakes occur when readers copy bibliographical details from the source to the request form. This can be as simple as confusing volume numbers with part numbers, or giving dates according to the US rather than the UK conventions.

Readers' handwriting can cause problems. Some libraries ask for a copy of the source of reference with the original request. Printed or typed requests are easier to deal with than handwritten ones, and some libraries encourage the use of Web-based requesting services for that reason alone.

Verification and location

Verification is the process of confirming that a book (or report or article) actually exists. Location is the process of identifying which libraries hold the book and may be willing to lend it. For most requests, the two processes are done simultaneously.

Verifying a request for IDS purposes is usually a matter of confirming or correcting the details given by the user, adding an ISBN if need be, and noting information which might help locate the material, for instance the fact that it is a monograph-in-series. If the citation turns out to need a lot of correcting, it is advisable to re-check the home library's catalogue, as it may be that the item is in fact in stock.

Books

A large number of books requested by UK readers will appear in the British Library Integrated Catalogue (BLIC). However, most books held in the Reference Division (St Pancras) are not available for loan. Therefore, many libraries first consult one of the union catalogues. Details of individual union catalogues are given in the Appendix.

There are two sorts of union catalogue – virtual union catalogues and databases. In a virtual union catalogue, the enquirer keys in the details once and the software searches a number of library OPACs simultaneously. The process may be fairly slow and the results will not be aggregated. So for a common title there may be a dozen returns or more. If the web-crawler cannot access a particular OPAC, it will provide no information about that library's holdings. Virtual searches often result in numerous 'false drops', particularly when searches are not done via ISBN. Virtual searches are very up to date – they search the target OPAC in real time and pick up the latest acquisitions. Examples of virtual union catalogues include the M25 Union Catalogue of Books, What's in London Libraries (WiLL), CAIRNS, RIDING and BOPAC. These catalogues are all available free of charge.

Union catalogues such as COPAC, UnityWeb and LinkUK (formerly Viscount)[4] rely on libraries notifying their holdings to a central database. Provided the catalogue records are compatible, a single record will be created with a list of holding libraries appended. 'False drops' are unusual. The search is usually executed much faster than on a virtual union catalogue. However, the database relies on libraries contributing data regularly. COPAC provides this information on its website. UnityWeb does not make the information publicly available, but it is clear that some libraries, particularly those of universities, have not updated their records for some years. The Combined Regions are attempting to address this problem by encouraging libraries to report regularly, on an agreed schedule. COPAC is available free of charge but UnityWeb and LinkUK are only available to subscribers. Very few libraries subscribe to both UnityWeb and LinkUK.[5] Although many public libraries report their holdings to LinkUK or UnityWeb, there are a number of university libraries and national collections which are not covered by any of the union catalogues.[6]

Most books will have been identified and located by this stage, and an application made to the BL or another supplier. How much further work is done will depend on the resources – time and access – available to the individual library. One useful tool for checking foreign publications, whether in English or other languages, is the Karlsruhe Virtual Catalogue. It is available free of charge over the Web and gives easy access to the catalogues of several dozen major libraries across the world. Academic libraries all have access to Worldcat through the JISC subscription; as well as providing an enormous amount of bibliographical data, this union catalogue gives information on the holdings of several UK libraries not covered by other sources. If union catalogues have been unsuccessful, a library may choose to check the printed catalogues or OPACs of libraries not covered by union catalogues. The London Library is worth considering alongside British university and public libraries. It is a private subscription library with excellent collections of material in the humanities and social sciences. Many UK libraries have 'representative membership', which allows them to borrow books for their readers. IDS staff report that it is a particularly good source for material published in the 19th or early 20th centuries.[7]

Books which do not appear in these sources may often be worth checking on ScholarGoogle, Google or any similar Internet search engine. Although UK location information will not be available, correct bibliographical data may emerge. Web searches will often show up articles in books which have been quoted as if they were books, spell out puzzling abbreviations, or provide the correct versions of names. The website of an individual publisher will give details of forthcoming books and allow a check on the backlist to establish whether a planned title was withdrawn.

When the BL carries out location searches, it will check some or all of these catalogues. It also has the remnants of the Union Catalogue of Books, which was started by the National Central Library. It may also check specialist catalogues such as the Slavonic Union Catalogue (on card) or the Oriental Union Catalogue (printed catalogue). The National Library of Scotland will check similar sources, plus CAIRNS and its own Scottish Union Catalogue, currently only available in card form.

Speculative approaches to individual libraries should be avoided unless you have good reason to believe they can help. For instance, many older university libraries have large collections of material which is only recorded in manual catalogues, or has not been catalogued at all.[8] If you – or your reader – are aware that a library has a good collection of material on a particular subject, but the book you need is not showing up on their OPAC, it may be worth a speculative approach. Public libraries often have locally published material in their collections which does not show up on union catalogues, but may still be available for loan. It is also acceptable to post speculative requests on mailing lists such as lis-ill (see Chapter 5).

Journals

Journal articles form the bulk of the IDS work done by many academic and special libraries. The BL's extensive holdings of journals mean that most applications to them for a journal article succeed immediately, and for this reason few institutions do much initial checking on article requests. However, some requests are obviously garbled and require attention; and if the BL sends a request back, it may be necessary to investigate it.

The main complications to be aware of are:

- There may be more than one journal with the same title. For instance, the Royal Institute of International Affairs in London publishes a well-known journal called *International Affairs*, but there is a Moscow journal of the same name. A management journal called *Omega* can be confused with a journal of the same title with a focus on death and dying. The journals are easily differentiated in the hand by their subtitles, and have different ISSNs, but the reader may not have such details in the reference. Looking at the subject of the articles can make it obvious which journal is required. SUNCAT can be a great help in sorting out these problems. It is also worth consulting the OPAC of libraries such as Cambridge University, which give a full list of issues received. For older journals, the printed volumes of the *British Union Catalogue of Periodicals (BUCOP)* or the *World List of Scientific Periodicals* can be very useful.

- The BL Newspaper Library does not have the resources to search through newspapers and weeklies to find an article, and insists on having page references. However, the reader's source may not give such detail, and many publications of this sort are not indexed. In these cases, it is worth contacting the other copyright libraries – Cambridge University Library, the Bodleian Library, National Library of Scotland, National Library of Wales and Trinity College Dublin. Specialist libraries such as the National Art Library at the Victoria and Albert Museum are often most helpful.

- Sometimes readers need to borrow whole issues of journals. The BL is the only library to allow this routinely. They will not lend journals until they have been in stock for 6 months.

- Journal titles are often abbreviated, either in the source or by the reader. There are a number of printed guides to journal title abbreviations. A quick check on the Internet may provide the full correct title. If in doubt, do not guess at the full form of the title but send the request to the BL in abbreviated form.

- The availability of online databases means that readers are now more aware of the range of literature on their subject and so may ask for more obscure titles. Conversely, the provision of electronic journals may mean that some readers limit themselves to consulting only those sources that are available online.

There are a number of general union catalogues of serials which supplement SUNCAT. However, it is worth being aware of specialist union lists. A number of useful resources, both online and printed, are listed in the Appendix.

Reports, official publications and grey literature

Reports, official publications and grey literature are notoriously difficult to control bibliographically, and enquiries need to be passed to specialist staff. The material can be hard to locate. However, the BL has vast collections of this material going back to the 1940s and earlier. Much of it is not fully listed in its publicly available catalogues. Sometimes it is recorded as serial entries under the name of the issuing body, so internal records or a shelf check are needed to establish exactly which items are available. In fact the BL can almost always supply British and US government publications, and documents from the United Nations, the European Union, the Organisation for Economic Co-operation and Development (OECD) and similar international bodies. When applying, it is important to give as much information as possible, including the precise issuing body and any series or reference numbers. A particular case in point is the vast and wide-ranging collection of American educational reports called 'ERIC'. There is a full set at the BL, on microfiche, and they arrive immediately if you can establish the ERIC ED number from the ERIC database, and quote it clearly in your request.

If the BL cannot help, it is often worth going to the organisation's homepage. You may be able to find enough additional information to reapply to the BL. It may be possible to download recent material from the website. Sometimes you can email the author of a report and request a copy.

Conference papers

Conference papers are important because they are often the first or only public report of a significant finding or of a new process or idea.

Researchers of all sorts, academics, postgraduate students, inventors and people working in industry often meet up to present their work and discuss it with other specialists. Small-scale events may be called workshops, symposia or seminars; larger events are usually called conferences and the very largest, often attracting hundreds of delegates, are called congresses. A large conference will have several sessions running in parallel, plus plenary sessions where all the delegates come together to hear important speakers. The formal sessions may be supplemented by 'Poster sessions', where people produce a summary of their work on one side of a sheet of paper, which is displayed in a large room. At a certain time, the poster producers can be found near their poster, so they can discuss their ideas with anyone who is interested.

Conferences may be single one-off events, but they are often held annually or at other planned intervals. They may be numbered. They usually move round to different venues. This is partly to give researchers from different parts of the country, or different parts of the world, the opportunity to attend the conference, partly to spread responsibility for organising the conference, partly to give delegates the chance to travel. To give some examples, the World Congress of Slavists is held at 5-yearly intervals, and has been held in locations such as Harrogate in Yorkshire, Warsaw and Banff in Canada. The International Federation of Library Associations has annual conferences – the 68th was held in Glasgow in 2002. One of the largest and most important organisers of conferences on technical topics is the US Institute of Electrical and Electronics Engineers. It is usually referred to as the IEEE (pronounced 'Eye – Triple E'). Conferences often have long and unwieldy titles, so may be referred to by an abbreviation – for instance ICDE2005 is the Institute of Electrical and Electronics Engineers' 21st International Conference on Data Engineering, 2005.

The posters and abstracts of the papers to be presented at the conference may be put together into a booklet, which is given to all the delegates on arrival. Sometimes this is the only permanent printed record of the conference. In addition, people presenting papers may bring copies with them, to give to other people expected to attend their session. These papers are often working documents, not polished for publication. Sometimes they are collected up and reproduced in their raw state. There may only be a couple of hundred copies produced. Alternatively, an editor may be appointed to select some of the conference papers, ask the authors to revise and update them, and then publish them as a book or as a special issue of a journal. For instance, 11 of the papers presented to the 43rd Annual Convention of the International Studies Association appeared in the *International Studies Review* vol. 5 part 4, 2003; many other papers presented to that conference do not appear to have been published anywhere at all. As a further complication, the person who presented the paper may revise it and publish it independently in a journal, or as a chapter in a book. The same raw material may well appear in several different guises in the years following its original presentation.

For IDS staff, the problems with conference papers include:

- *Long complicated citations.* Citations for conference papers are often lengthy and involve abbreviations. Readers may need to produce a copy of their source of reference at an early stage for IDS staff to identify the conference required. It can be difficult to squeeze all the information into a standard BL application form.

- *Was it published?* The paper may not be included in the published volume arising out of the conference. Other people may quote the paper on the basis of the circulated document, but it is not in the public domain. A careful search of specialist bibliographies may reveal that the author published an article on the same area in a mainstream journal, and that may be enough for the reader. Otherwise the only hope to get hold of it then is to contact the author direct.

Bibliographical information

The BL has one of the world's best collections of conference literature, which has been built up since the 1950s. Bibliographical information about its holdings is available in BLIC. Many conference proceedings – because they appear regularly – are treated as serials by the BL, so you will find the record in BLIC is just an open entry indicating when the holdings start and finish. So a search for a precise conference title may fail whereas a search on the issuing body may succeed. However, BLIC only lists the proceedings not the individual papers within the proceedings. For this you need a more detailed bibliographical source, such as *British Library Direct* or *ZETOC*. This includes the BL's own index to conference proceedings, and covers holdings from the mid-1990s onwards. It is possible to search by title, author and conference details. You will then be able to obtain a detailed citation, and the BL shelfmark. For earlier years, there is the *Index to Conference Proceedings Received*, which began in 1964.

Subject databases can be useful for dealing with conference papers. Many include the BL shelf number in their bibliographical information. The most widely used online sources for science and technology conferences are probably EDINA, INSPEC and Web of Science. The IEEE website can now be searched for bibliographical data free of charge, although payment is required to access the documents found.

Standards and patents

Enquiries about standards and patents are best referred to specialist staff. For IDS purposes, the main source of information about standards in the UK is the British Standards Institute (BSI), which has a large collection of UK and foreign standards. However, it does not lend its UK standards. These can usually be borrowed from the BL in the normal way. The BL has some foreign standards, but if they cannot supply they will suggest the BSI. The BSI lends to its members, who buy books of library tokens that are used to pay for loans. In addition, many large public libraries have significant collections of standards and are an alternative source of supply.

Patents are available from a number of large public libraries, notably Leeds Public Library (apply to LD/P-2).

Theses and dissertations

Theses and dissertations are the written documents produced by students at the end of a higher degree or as part of their undergraduate studies. They are often of great interest to other researchers because they may:

- be the first or only discussion of a particular topic,
- contain details not given in published articles resulting from the thesis,
- treat certain aspects of the subject in greater depth than is possible in a publication.

UK theses

Generally no more than three or four copies of the typescript are produced and bound, usually by the university bindery. Older theses may be carbon copies of the author's typescript. Sometimes a dissertation or thesis may contain material that is commercially, politically or personally sensitive. In these cases the library may have a copy but will only release it to a reader in person, on the production of the written permission of the author or of the author's department. Such restrictions are usually indicated in the institution's OPAC.

Undergraduate dissertations

Many undergraduate students write a dissertation, typically of about 10,000 words, in the final year of their course. Undergraduate dissertations do not normally contain original material. University libraries seldom hold undergraduate dissertations and many departments do not have them either. They are not listed in bibliographies and indexes. However, they may occasionally be cited by the author or by others. In general the only way of acquiring a copy is to make contact with the student direct. In some cases the department may have an address on file, or be willing to forward a request.

Taught courses

Most taught postgraduate courses require the submission of a dissertation after 1 or 2 years of study. Many MA, MSc and MBA courses fall into this category. The dissertation is often limited to about 20,000 words. At this level the dissertation may be seen as evidence of the ability to carry out research, or a preliminary assessment of the research potential of a topic, rather than original research. Some universities do require students to deposit a copy of their dissertation with the university library, and others keep a copy in the department. Some universities arrange for the deposit of good dissertations in order to provide an example for subsequent students. However, many universities do not appear to have any system for even recording the titles of the dissertations submitted to them. It follows that the bibliographical control of such dissertations is not systematic, although some are listed in *Index to theses*. However, where general sources fail they may sometimes be traced through specialist bibliographies on particular subjects.

Research

Theses and dissertations produced by students working for a research degree are expected to make an original contribution to knowledge, albeit frequently in a very specialist niche. They are typically between 80,000 and 100,000 words long and represent a substantial investment of time and intellectual resources. Nomenclature for higher degrees varies between universities, but generally an MPhil thesis is less substantial than that presented for PhD or DPhil. The bibliographical control of theses at this level is the responsibility of *Index to theses*. Records are available online for 1970 onwards, and in paper form from 1950. Universities are expected to notify the compilers of PhD, DPhil and MPhil theses awarded by their institution, and authors of theses at lower levels do often advise *Index to theses* of their work.

Work in progress

Theses and dissertations can take many years to prepare. Problems arise for interlending staff when our readers assert that a thesis has been written by a student at a particular university and we can find no trace of the thesis in that institution's OPAC or elsewhere. In these cases the best we can do is contact IDS staff to see if they can ascertain the status of the work, or try to contact the author direct.

Copyright

British theses are not published documents, and so the author's copyright has to be protected by library staff when giving access to the thesis. There is more information on copyright in Chapter 11.

British Library

The BL has copies of over 165,000 British PhD/DPhil theses, from 1970 onwards. At one time the BL filmed all PhD/DPhil theses automatically, but this became too expensive. Now theses are microfilmed on demand, provided the university that awarded the degree takes part in the thesis microfilming scheme. Records for most UK theses held appear on the BL catalogue, and the BL is happy to respond to any enquiry about the availability of a particular thesis. Libraries may borrow the microfilm or purchase a bound printout of the thesis. A number of British universities require the reader to sign a Thesis Declaration Form (TDF); this must be submitted to the BL before the film will be sent. This requirement is reflected in the order number given to the thesis: those with the order number preceded by DX do not need a TDF; those preceded by D require one. Full details of the BL British thesis service are available on the BL website. Some British universities have withdrawn from the BL's thesis copying scheme, and now supply all requests for theses which are not already on microfilm at the BL. These include Bradford and Manchester. An up-to-date list is available on the BL website.

Loans

Although many requests for theses can be satisfied from the BL, many libraries do wish to borrow a hard copy of a thesis. Most readers prefer to work from a paper copy in the library rather than having to use microfilm. Other reasons include:

- Thesis out of BL scope – e.g. MBA or MPhil.
- Thesis awarded by an institution not participating in the BL microfilming scheme.
- Thesis not yet filmed by the BL. As it can take weeks or even months to get a film made, borrowing the original is attractive. However, some libraries never lend their PhDs and will refer all requests to the BL.
- Maps, drawings and illustrations do not reproduce well on microfilm.
- Reader is visually impaired and cannot read microfilm.
- Reader does not have access to a microfilm reader.

There is considerable variation between universities in their policies on lending theses. Some libraries have two copies of theses and make one available for loan. In the case of the University of London, one copy of the thesis is retained by the School or College where the student was based, and is not available for loan. The second copy is sent to the University of London Library in Senate House (LO/U-1), and is available for loan. The theses loan policies of all UK universities are summarised on the FIL website.

Copies

Many libraries are willing to make photocopies or other copies of theses for readers. However, there are variations in policy on whether the author's permission must be sought in advance, or a signed TDF sent with the request. In many cases it may be better to order a copy from BLDSC. Their copies are bound and may be available more rapidly and at lower cost than from the university library.

Electronic theses

At present British universities do not store or make available their theses in electronic format, although this is done in certain other countries. There are copyright problems as well as technological issues to be addressed. The 'Theses Alive' project has now resulted in a plan (announced April 2005) to make UK theses available electronically from the BL.[9]

Foreign theses

Theses in Scandinavia, Germany and much of Western Europe are produced as books, albeit with a very small print run. The awarding university will often lend, for International Federation of Library Associations (IFLA) vouchers. Proquest Digital Dissertations, which grew out of *Dissertations Abstracts International*, lists US and Canadian doctoral theses; it has recently begun to include those from a number of other countries including Australia, New Zealand, Hong Kong, China and Spain. The BL bought many US theses produced before 2001, which are stored on microfiche. At present they are not listed on BLIC and the only way to find out if the BL holds them is to apply, quoting the thesis reference number (AAT) and putting US Thesis in the STATUS box. Most US theses can be purchased direct from Proquest Digital Dissertations; the more recent ones are instantly available in PDF format. Many US universities will not copy or lend theses which are available through Proquest Digital Dissertations. However, masters' theses and other theses not available via Proquest may be provided. A direct approach to the university's ILL service will usually get a prompt and helpful response. Canadian PhD theses can be borrowed from the National Library of Canada, on microfiche, for a small fee. Australia is a pioneer in the area of electronic theses and if you look up a thesis on the OPAC you may find a link through to the full text. Otherwise a direct approach to the university library's ILL department is often successful.

Market reports

Readers often want access to market reports and other very expensive collections of data aimed at commercial users. The BL does receive a copy of all UK publications of this sort under Legal Deposit, but retains them in the Business Information Service, for library use only. Any copies in the other copyright libraries will be subject to the same restrictions. The reader will have to be advised to travel to the sources.

Psychological testing material

Educationalists, clinical psychologists and psychologists sometimes want psychological tests – the manuals, test materials, instructions on interpretation, etc. However, access to such material is generally restricted by the publishers, as it must be used only by those trained to carry out such tests. It does sometimes appear on COPAC, as the University of London's Senate House Library (LO/U-1) houses the British Psychological Society's Library, but this material is never lent. If the reader is in an appropriate profession, he or she may be able to get access to the material through a university department or the local authority's educational psychology service.

Fiction

Readers often want to read novels which are not held in their own library. Many public libraries have a policy of purchasing in print fiction when requested. This is partly because of the relative costs of purchase against interlending, partly because it is often faster. Furthermore, many public libraries will not lend recent fiction on IDS, or will not lend any fiction titles unless the author is part of their responsibility under the Joint Fiction Reserve (see below).

However, when a fiction request comes through to interlending, there are a number of questions to bear in mind:

- *Does the reader need a particular edition of the book?* A reader may ask for the 1935 edition of a book, because he or she knows that is when it was first published, but may be just as happy with a 1980s edition. On the other hand, a student may need a particular edition because of the introduction by a particular scholar, or an edition with good footnotes. Be aware that some editions of books are abridged or bowdlerized, and this may matter to your reader.

- *Is the US title the same as the British title?* Sometimes a book will appear with completely different titles in different parts of the English-speaking world. It can be very difficult to establish this without having both books together.

- *Is it translated?* People reading translated fiction may specify a particular translator, for instance the Constance Garnett editions of Russian novels rather than more recent ones. The same book can be translated under several different titles.

- *Can I borrow it from the BL?* The BL holds an archive copy of all novels published in the UK, but they are not available for loan. The BL does not purchase children's or adult fiction. However, it may well hold critical editions of literary works. In addition, it inherited quite a lot of fiction from the National Central Library.

- *Other copyright libraries.* The copyright libraries – Cambridge, Oxford, National Library of Scotland, National Library of Wales and Trinity College Dublin – may acquire copies of novels for their collections. They are often not fully catalogued and will not be recorded in union catalogues such as COPAC. When searching for British novels more than 5 years old it is always worth a speculative approach to Cambridge in particular. However, the copyright libraries lend for library use only.

- *What about other libraries?* Many libraries report their holdings on COPAC, UnityWeb or LinkUK, and you may find locations for fiction there. You can then apply in the normal way.

- *Joint Fiction Reserves.* The first Joint Fiction Reserve (JFR) began in London and the South East in 1946. It was adopted in the rest of England in 1962. The JFR for the Republic of Ireland and Northern Ireland was established in 1965. Different public libraries take on responsibility for certain authors, and undertake to retain copies of 'their' authors' works. For instance, authors named D-Davies were the responsibility of Sunderland in the England scheme, of Greenwich within LASER, and of the North Eastern Education and Library Board in Ireland. However, the effectiveness of the JFR always varied according to the level of commitment which individual public libraries could give it. In recent years, many libraries and regions have cut back on their JFR collections, and some have been dispersed. Nevertheless, some collections are still in existence, and speculative approaches to the appropriate library can often be successful. The Yorkshire and Humberside JFR in Wakefield is particularly helpful. The Scottish Fiction Reserve was set up in 1955 to ensure the availability of Scottish authors' works; public libraries undertook to collect books by authors with local connections. The National Library of Scotland's Inter Library Services can direct enquiries to the appropriate library. The most recent *Guide to the Joint Fiction Reserves* was produced in 1999 and can be downloaded from the Conarls website. Many of the JFR collections are not listed in online catalogues and so will not appear in UnityWeb or LinkUK.

- *Children's literature.* IDS is unlikely to be called in to supply children's literature for children, but there are many adults – in higher education and elsewhere – who are interested in studying children's books. Children's literature was included in the JFR scheme. In addition, the Yorkshire and Humberside Region in Wakefield built up a Junior Fiction collection. Few libraries (other than the copyright libraries) keep pre-1945 children's books. Sometimes you may find that they are held in special collections, such as those at Manchester Metropolitan University or the Centre for the Book at the University of Northumbria, so are not available for loan.

Foreign-language publications

Two sorts of requests can be discussed here: (a) provision of material for readers wanting to read ethnic minority languages, and (b) material in foreign languages for readers whose first language is English.

Union catalogues sometimes list material in ethnic minority languages. In addition, IDS librarians will sometimes appeal on sources such as the UnityWeb mailing list for selections of books in particular languages, for instance 'Can anyone lend us five modern fiction books in Albanian'. However, a better solution may be to rent books from a supplier such as Bright Books. They hire out collections of books in minority languages to public libraries, and will put together a selection of books such as 'Children's books in Lithuanian'. They maintain records of which books have been provided to which library so that a further selection includes fresh material. The Polish Library in London provides a similar service for Polish-language material.

Despite the UK's reputation as a monoglot nation, many of our readers want material in languages other than English. For the IDS librarian, the main priorities are:

- Ensure the request is legible.

- Have it in the original language, not in translation.[10] If it is not in Latin script, ask for the text in transliteration.

- Make sure that the reader realises that the publication is in a foreign language. Many databases provide an English translation of the article title and an English abstract, and the reader can easily overlook the note that says 'In Portuguese'. If you apply to the BL and are unsure whether the article is in English or not, you can put TRANSON as the Message Keyword to indicate that you want it only if it can be supplied in English; to indicate that the reader would prefer it in English, put TRANSIP.

COPAC is an excellent source of information about foreign publications. The BL will often lend foreign books held at St Pancras, for library use only. The National Library of Scotland is also ready to lend many of the foreign publications it has purchased, for library use only. If 'Oxford' is given as a location, make sure you check whether the book is in the Bodleian Library (OX/U-1), the Taylor Institution (OX/U19) or another collection.

If you cannot find the work in COPAC, you will need to verify the bibliographical details before trying further. Worldcat is useful if you have access to it; otherwise you can search many National Libraries simultaneously from the Karlsruhe Virtual Catalogue (KVK). IFLA provides a list of the main union catalogues in individual foreign countries. Those in France and Germany are particularly useful. Beyond that, it is worth trying to find the OPAC for university libraries in the region or country concerned – Libweb index is a good starting point. Many have an English-language version of their website available. The mechanics of borrowing from abroad are discussed in Chapter 12.

Music

Lending and borrowing music is an important service to performing musicians, as well as to people who listen to or study music.[11] In some local authorities the Music Library operates separately to the rest of the library, and so music requests are dealt with by specialist staff rather than the IDS unit. In most higher education libraries and in many public libraries music requests are dealt with by IDS staff, who often find them a challenge. The International Association of Music Libraries runs courses on interlending music, which demystify the terminology and help staff deal with music requests. There is a lot of information on the National Library of Scotland's Web pages, which will be useful for librarians in the rest of the UK as well as those in Scotland. In addition, Libraries NorthWest (LNW) has just embarked on a Music and Drama Project, which aims to bring together information for IDS librarians on all aspects of music and drama interlending, including guidelines on good practice. There are details on its website.

The different forms of music which may be requested are:

- Full or orchestral score – displays each instrumental or vocal part on a separate line, as needed by the conductor of a performance. Usually a large format publication.

- Miniature score – a pocket-sized version of the full or orchestral score, enabling a performance to be followed by a listener or studied.

- Vocal score – each vocal part of an opera or choral work, i.e. soprano, alto, tenor and bass, with accompanying score or piano reduction.
- Instrumental music for solo instruments, or for a combination of instruments such as a string quartet.
- Part – music for one instrument or voice in an ensemble.
- Orchestral set – a full score plus all the instrumental parts required to perform a work.
- Vocal set – the vocal scores or choral parts a choir needs to perform a work.

Borrowing miniature scores or full scores is relatively straightforward. Many are listed in union catalogues such as COPAC. The BL has a full collection of UK published music scores at St Pancras, for reference use. In addition, BLDSC has a large collection of music scores available for loan. The collection is not yet on BLIC, but speculative approaches are welcome. Put MUSIC in the status box.

Performance sets

Borrowing performance sets is more difficult. There is a great deal of information and advice in Malcolm Lewis's book, although it does not cover online resources.[12] He includes very useful lists of abbreviations and musical terms in different languages.

The first step is to establish what the requester wants:

- How long the music will be needed, i.e. when rehearsals start and when the performance will be held.
- Composer's name.
- Title of the work. Check whether it has a popular name as well as a formal name, and whether there is an Opus number or catalogue number. If it is part of a larger work, try to get details of both. If the title is in a foreign language, try to get the name by which it is known in English too. For instance, Haydn's 'Paukenmesse' is also known as his 'Kettle Drum Mass' and 'Mass in Time of War'.
- Arrangement required, e.g. 'arrangement for wind band' or 'SATB' – which means arranged for soprano, alto, tenor and bass.
- Editor and publisher. Editions prepared by different editors or printed by different publishers can vary widely, so check what is required.

If you need to borrow an orchestral set for a choral performance it is vital to have the same edition of the vocal score and the orchestral set.

- Number of copies required. If you are borrowing an orchestral set, the number of copies will be determined by the arrangement. For a vocal set you will need to know how many copies the choir needs.

There are a number of printed catalogues of orchestral sets and vocal sets which have not been entirely superseded by online resources, and they are listed on the National Library of Scotland website and on the LNW website. However, the first place to look is the online database Encore, produced by the International Association of Music Librarians in the UK and Ireland, and accessible from their website.

Most libraries which lend orchestral sets and vocal scores make a charge equivalent to double the normal BL loan charge, to cover the additional transport and administrative costs. However, several large and important music collections do not lend through the BL system. Westminster, Liverpool and Manchester public libraries, for instance, lend only to subscribers. Hull and Kent public libraries, and the Yorkshire Libraries Joint Music and Drama Service in Wakefield, lend to UK libraries, but do not accept payment through the BL 'Banker Scheme' and have to be paid on invoice. Whatever the source, it is normal practice to telephone to enquire about the availability of a set before making a written application. The conditions of the loan can be clarified then.

Some music is not available for loan through the library service. This includes a great deal of recent music. In this case, the options available include:

- Borrow it from another society through the Online Music Exchange Service of the National Federation of Music Societies.
- Hire from the publishers or music shops. The Music Publishers Association website provides useful links.

Again, the LNW website provides useful links.

Play sets

Play sets are available from a number of public libraries, and from societies and commercial suppliers. There are fuller details of many of these sources on the LNW website.

Maps

There is no central interlending service for maps. In addition they are often too fragile, large and unwieldy to send to other libraries. In many cases, it may be more appropriate to advise the reader to use the Web to access the images required.

Maps are covered on COPAC – there is the option to search the database for maps alone. The UK's copyright libraries all have large collections of maps, both UK and foreign. The BL's collection is accessible in a separate map catalogue on their website. The National Library of Scotland is in the process of converting its map catalogue, so some material is listed in the main NLS OPAC; the remaining records are in a card catalogue. Further information is available from the Map Library.

Copying recent British maps is restricted by the Ordnance Survey. There is further information on their website.

However, in many cases users do not need paper copies of maps as they can find what they need over the Web. A large number of institutions are now making historical maps from their collections available in digital form. The BL and the National Library of Scotland have particularly useful collections. In addition, the Ordnance Survey now provides the Digimap Service. Users in UK higher education institutions have access to it through EDINA, and many public libraries can use it via local authority licensing agreements.

Audio-visual materials

Videos, CD-ROMs, DVDs, CDs and audio cassettes pose many problems for inter-library loans staff. These include:

- limited bibliographical control and union catalogue information;
- copyright regulations and licensing agreements which prevent the library which owns the item from lending it to non-members;
- variations in physical format, susceptibility to damage, and the need for special equipment to view/use the material.

Details of some libraries' holdings of films, videos, DVDs, CDs, audio-cassettes, etc., do appear in COPAC, UnityWeb, LinkUK and other union catalogues.

Audio recordings

The Greater London Audio Specialisation Scheme (GLASS) began in 1972 as an attempt to ensure that at least one copy of all gramophone recordings produced in the UK was available within the London region. The scheme started with classical, jazz and spoken word records and was later enlarged to include folk music and, eventually, CDs. Each London Borough has set responsibilities; details may be found by going to the CECILIA website and searching under GLASS. Records for some GLASS holdings are listed in LinkUK (formerly Viscount) or on WiLL. Speculative requests for CDs and other recordings are accepted. Initially the scheme was for libraries in the Greater London area but applications for loans are now welcome from other parts of the UK.[13]

Videos and DVDs

Where a video has been made for retail sale, prices are often very reasonable and it may be better to suggest your library purchases the item. Although some institutions never lend videos and DVDs, others will, provided the material has been purchased commercially rather than acquired under the Educational Recording Agency (ERA) licence. You may be able to check on a library's policies from their website or regional listings. The ERA licence scheme is run by the British Universities Film and Video Council (BUFVC). Nearly all UK further and higher education institutions have an ERA licence, and through BUFVC membership are entitled to a certain number of recordings free each year. The BUFVC runs TRILT: the Television and Radio Index for Learning and Teaching, and maintains an archive of important television broadcasts. The BUFVC also offers HERMES, an online database of videos and DVDs available in the UK, with details of their suppliers.

The British Film Institute (BFI) library takes part in normal interlending work, particularly as a source for photocopies of journal articles. However, its collections of films are not available through the ILL system. Their website gives access to their catalogue of films available for hire, and to their sales catalogue of films and DVDs.

BEE Aware and services for visually impaired people

Audio-cassettes, DVDs, books in Moon and Braille, and large print books intended for visually impaired people are listed in the REVEAL database. (REVEAL is also available through UnityWeb.) The LNW Business Unit provides full information on the BEE Aware interlending service on its Web pages.

And finally ...

IDS work brings you into contact with a very wide range of material, and very few people can deal with it all unaided. Many IDS staff work in small units, or have little specialist training. However, there is usually someone 'out there' who has dealt with a similar problem before, or may be able to access resources that you cannot. You may have a mentor in your own library, or a person you met on a training course. If not, it is always worth asking the wider interlending community for help. There are several email mailing lists, including those provided by UnityWeb and LinkUK, and by some of the regional library services. Anyone can join the mailing list lis-ill (see Chapter 5), and colleagues often ask there for help locating publications or sorting out queries.

Appendix: websites

OPACs

Higher education institutions *http://www.hero.ac.uk/niss/niss_library4008 .cfm*
Public libraries *http://www.harden.dial.pipex.com/weblibs.html*
London Library *http://www.londonlibrary.co.uk*
Worldwide: Libweb Index *http://lists.webjunction.org/libweb/*

Union catalogues

COPAC *http://www.copac.ac.uk*
BOPAC *http://www.bopac2.comp.brad.ac.uk/~bopac2/egwcgi.cgi/egwirtcl/ mtargets.egw/1+0*
M25 (London) *http://www.m25lib.ac.uk/Link/*
Riding (Yorkshire plus) *http://riding.hostedbyfdi.net/riding/index.html*
CAIRNS (Scotland) *http://cairns.lib.strath.ac.uk/*
WiLL (London Public Libraries) *http://www.londonlibraries.org.uk/will/ Categories.aspx*

IFLA List of Union Catalogues *http://www.ifla.org/VI/2/duc/index.htm*
Karlsruhe Virtual Catalogue *http://www.ubka.uni-karlsruhe.de/hylib/en/ kvk.html*

Serials union catalogues

SUNCAT *http://edina.ac.uk/suncat/*
LAMDA *http://lamda.mimas.ac.uk/*
SALSER *http://edina.ed.ac.uk/salser/*
M25 *http://www.m25lib.ac.uk/ULS/*
ABTAPL – Theological and Philosophical Libraries *http://www.le.ac.uk/ abtapl/aba.html*
Italian journals *http://ipcat.leeds.ac.uk*
Libraries NorthWest *http://www.lnw.org.uk/periodicals/index.asp*
ARLIS (art journals) *http://ipac.nal.vam.ac.uk/ipac20/ipac.jsp?profile =arlisnet#focusfocus*

Standards

http://www.bsi-global.com

Patents

http://www.patent.gov.uk/
http://www.bl.uk/services/document/patent.html

Theses

British Library *http://www.bl.uk/britishthesis*
UK universities lending policies *http://www.cilip.org.uk/groups/fil/ theses.html*
Proquest Digital Dissertations *http://wwwlib.umi.com/dissertations/ gateway*

Fiction – Joint Fiction Reserve

http://www.thenortheast.com/conarls/JFRguide.pdf

Foreign language publications

Bright Books *http://www.brightbooks.co.uk*
The Polish Library in London *http://www.posk.org.uk*

Music

Libraries North West *http://www.lnw.org.uk/bu/music/musicintro.asp*
International Association of Music Libraries UK and Ireland *http://www.iaml-uk-irl.org*
National Library of Scotland *http://www.nls.uk/professional/interlibraryservices/services/music_interlending.html*
Encore *http://www.iaml-uk.org/*
Cecilia *http://www.cecilia-uk.org/html/*
Music Publishers Association *http://www.mpaonline.org.uk*

Maps

British Library *http://www.bl.uk/collections/maps.html*
Ordnance Survey *http://www.ordnancesurvey.co.uk*
National Library of Scotland *http://www.nls.uk/maps*
Further information *http://oddens.geog.uu.nl/index.html, http://www.maphistory.info/*

Audio-visual material

British Universities Film and Video Council *http://www.bufvc.ac.uk*
British Film Institute *http://www.bfi.org.uk*
Revealweb *http://www.revealweb.org.uk*

Notes

1. Parry, David (1997) *Why requests fail: interlibrary lending and document supply request failures in the UK and Ireland. A report to CONARLS.* Newcastle: Information North for CONARLS (British Library Research and Innovation Centre Project, Report 59) (0906433258).
2. This is not new; apparently Dr Urquhart used to joke that 'two of the most heavily demanded titles in the NLL are 'Private Communication' and 'In

Progress'. Watson, Peter G. (1970) *Great Britain's National Lending Library.* Los Angeles: University of California School of Library Service, p. 59.

3. For example, the obituary of Bas Pease in *The Times* on 26 October 2004 states 'In 1955, he published, with George Kinchin, a key scientific paper on the mechanism of damage to solids [...]. The paper is a classic in its field'. Identifying the correct citation required a physics specialist as well as an experienced librarian!

4. LinkUK records are now being added to the OCLC database Worldcat too.

5. Some indication of the reasons behind this is given in: Hendrix, Frances (2004) 'You may think that I could not possibly comment: a personal view of resource sharing in the UK over recent years along with major events that have impeded progress', *Interlending and Document Supply* 32(3): 176–82.

6. As of July 2005, LinkUK had 78 subscribing members in the UK; UnityWeb includes data from hundreds of libraries but a significant number do not seem to update their records regularly.

7. *Catalogue of the London Library.* London: Williams & Norgat, 1903–68, 8 volumes. For more recent material, consult the website at: *http://www. londonlibrary.co.uk*

8. Around 14 million items, according to the CURL *Survey of outstanding material for retrospective conversion and retrospective cataloguing in CURL libraries.* 2004.

9. See also: Copeland, Susan and Penman, Andrew (2004) 'The development and promotion of electronic theses and dissertations within the UK', *The New Review of Information Networking* 10(1): 19–32.

10. We once applied to the BL for an article from a French journal which our reader had told us was called 'The Weekly Barber'. Puzzled response from BL. When we got her source of reference, it turned out to be in the *Figaro Hebdomadaire* – the weekly published by the French newspaper called *Le Figaro*. The barber came (I guess) from the opera character called Figaro, who is a barber.

11. The background is explained in: Thompson, Pamela (1994) 'Music and interlending in the United Kingdom', *Interlending and Document Supply*, 22(4): 4–7.

12. Lewis, Malcolm (1989) *Sets of Vocal Music: a Librarian's Guide to Interlending Practice.* London: IAML UK (095023396X).

13. I am most grateful to Ruth Hellen of Enfield Public Libraries for information about GLASS.

8

Management systems for interlending and document supply

Stephen Prowse

Introduction

Traditionally, writers on library management systems (LMS) have tended to focus on a limited number of themes – system procurement, system functionality as a whole or the functionality of particular modules. Although such topics have their merits, there are a number of dimensions being overlooked. These include the worth of drawing up detailed system specifications, what do you do with an interlending and document supply (IDS) system once you have got it, how will it be developed and how can existing customers influence development? It is on these neglected aspects that I will concentrate, rather than revisiting familiar territory. Similarly, I will not describe any system in detail, other than itemising some key information. Table 8.1 provides an overview of what I consider to be the important features.

A number of writers have covered procurement and implementation so I will not dwell long on these topics. Readers are advised to refer to Myhill,[1] who gives an overview of the whole process from the viewpoint of an academic library – Exeter University.

Additionally, if we look at IDS in particular, in the major decision to purchase an LMS, and in which one to choose, the functionality and performance of the IDS module will rate a considerable way behind circulation, cataloguing, the OPAC, etc. And once the system has been bought, installed, used and found to be not quite the perfect solution as promised or expected, what can be done? Whatever its faults, the system will be around for several years and you will just have to live with it.

Table 8.1 Overview of Library Management Systems

Company	Product/ ILL	Product website	Main countries outside UK	Main markets	Software upgrades	ISO ILL? Tested with BL?	Bug reporting	Bug fixes	User group?	How may customers influence development?
Stand-alone systems										
Christie Hospital	WinC HILL	http://www.winchill.co.uk/	–	Academic, Medical	Irregular	N – planned for version 9 in 2006	Via help desk	Program sent to customer	Y	Direct & via user group. Bespoke development at small cost if not widely beneficial
Clio Software	Clio	http://cliosoftware.com/public/	USA, Canada, Australia	Academic, Public	2 a year	Y & BL	Email to technical support	Major ones by new release, minor ones in next scheduled release	Y – email list & regional meetings	Regional meetings (in US), email list, direct feedback
Fretwell-Downing Informatics	VDX (see also OLIB7)	http://www.fdgroup.com/fdi/products/vdx4.html	Austra-lasia, North America	Academic, National, Public	18 months	Y & BL	Online, help desk	Via patches - rapid deployment for urgent fixes	Y	Via user group & workshops. Requests go into a 'Problems & Requirements' List. Internal evaluation then voting by user groups

Table 8.1 Overview of Library Management Systems (*Cont'd*)

Company	Product/ ILL	Product website	Main countries outside UK	Main markets	Software upgrades	ISO ILL? Tested with BL?	Bug reporting	Bug fixes	User group?	How may customers influence development?
Lancaster University	ILLOS	http://www.illos .lancs.ac.uk/	–	Academic, Public	Irregular	N but new ILLOS in development	Via support desk	Installed remotely or via email	Y	Enhancement requests added to development schedule (informal)
RLG	ILL Manager	http://www.rlg.org/ en/page .php?Page_ID=345	USA	Academic	2 a year	Y & BL	Via the RLG Information Center	In next update, or sent to individual site or downloadable from website	Y (in US)	Direct then evaluated
ILMS										
Autolib	Autolib	http://www.autolib .co.uk	–	Education, Special	1 a year	N	Direct	Downloadable from website	Online forum	Direct feedback, can provide at cost to customers or reduced cost if widespread applicability
Bailey Solutions	KnowAll, Konduct	http://www .baileysolutions .co.uk/	–	Corporate, Special	1 a year	N	Email to support	Downloadable from website	Y – annual meeting & email list	Direct feedback – added to development schedule

Table 8.1 Overview of Library Management Systems (*cont'd*)

Company	Product/ ILL	Product website	Main countries outside UK	Main markets	Software upgrades	ISO ILL? Tested with BL?	Bug reporting	Bug fixes	User group?	How may customers influence development?
Bibliomondo	Concerto, Portfolio (about to sell in UK)	*http://www .bibliomondo.com/*	Europe; France, Canada, North America	Public; Academic, Corporate	2 a year; 2 a year	N; Y not BL	Online, help desk	Via updates or patches	Y	Via user group, regular visits. Development can be for individual customers
DS	Open-Galaxy/ Xchange	*http://www.ds.co .uk/*	–	Public	1 a year	Y not BL	Via central help desk	Delivered remotely to server	ILL Special Interest Group	Focus group, special interest group and via placing requests for enhancement with the DS Help Desk
Dynix*	Horizon, Corinthi-an/URSA (Universal Resource Sharing Appli-cation)	*http://www.dynix .com/products/*	World-wide	Horizon to be for Public, Corinthian for Academic	Every 12–18 months	Y & BL	Online, help desk	Interim releases & individual fixes	Y	Via annual and regional meetings. Via user group – weighted voting to counter country bias

Table 8.1 Overview of Library Management Systems (*cont'd*)

Company	Product/ ILL	Product website	Main countries outside UK	Main markets	Software upgrades	ISO ILL? Tested with BL?	Bug reporting	Bug fixes	User group?	How may customers influence development?
Endeavor	Voyager	http://www .endinfosys.com/ prods/ill.htm	North America, Australia	Academic	2 a year	Y & BL	Via support desk	In next release or via patches if urgent	Y	Via user group & also direct feedback
Ex Libris	Aleph 500	http://www.exlibris .co.il/aleph_ILL .htm	World-wide	Academic, Public, National	1 a year	Y – currently testing with the BL	Online	Via service packs	Y	Via national and international user groups. Focus groups.
Fretwell-Downing Informatics	OLIB7	http://www.fdgroup .com/fdi/products/ olib4.html	Europe, Middle East, Columbia	Academic, Corporate, Special	1 a year	Y & BL	Online, help desk	Via patches – rapid deployment for urgent fixes	Y	Via user group & workshops. Requests go into a 'Problems & Requirements' List. Internal evaluation then voting by user groups

Table 8.1   Overview of Library Management Systems (*cont'd*)

Company	Product/ ILL	Product website	Main countries outside UK	Main markets	Software upgrades	ISO ILL? Tested with BL?	Bug reporting	Bug fixes	User group?	How may customers influence development?
Geac	Advance, Vubis Smart	http://www.library .geac.com/page /products_LIB.html	World-wide	Advance – Public in US, Academic in UK (NB. Vubis Smart only system now sold – Public, Academic, Special)	2 a year, 1 a year from 2006	N – planned for 2006	Online	Priority fixes, patches or next general release	Y	Direct, via user group & ILL focus group. Internal evaluation. Bespoke development at cost for Advance
Infovision Technology	Amlib	http://www. infovision-tech.com/	Australia, New Zealand, South Africa, USA	Education, Special	1 a year	N	Direct	Downloadable from website	N but has email list	Direct then evaluated – may already be in the pipeline

Table 8.1 Overview of Library Management Systems (cont'd)

Company	Product/ ILL	Product website	Main countries outside UK	Main markets	Software upgrades	ISO ILL? Tested with BL?	Bug reporting	Bug fixes	User group?	How may customers influence development?
Innovative Interfaces	Millenni-um/INN-Reach Direct Consor-tial Borrowing	http://www.iii.com/mill/index.shtml	World-wide	Academic	1 a year	Y & BL	Via help desk	By connecting to customers' systems	Y	Enhancement requests direct or through user groups – then vote & implement highest ranking in each module
IS Oxford	Heritage IV – ILL module in develop-ment	http://www.isoxford.com/home.php	–	Academic, Corporate, Medical, Legal	2 a year	NA		Downloadable ad hoc patches	Y	Via user group & Support Services
Sirsi*	Unicorn	http://www.sirsi.co.uk/unicorn.htm	World-wide	Academic, Legal, Museum, Public, Special	1 a year	Y & BL	Email, phone	Via patches	Y	Online forum for suggestions, user voting. Bespoke development at cost
Softlink	Liberty3, Oliver	http://www.softlink.co.uk/	World-wide	Corporate, Special	1 a year	N	To support team	Via special releases	Y email list	Direct – can pay part of cost of development work to accelerate development

Table 8.1   Overview of Library Management Systems (cont'd)

Company	Product/ILL	Product website	Main countries outside UK	Main markets	Software upgrades	ISO ILL? Tested with BL?	Bug reporting	Bug fixes	User group?	How may customers Influence development?
Soutron	2020, Soutron.l MS (now incorporated into Inmagic Genie)	http://www.soutron.com/	–	Legal, NHS, Non-profit, Finance	1 a year	Y & BL for 2020, N for Soutron.l MS	Via help desk – online tracking system	Upgrades for general use or specific use	Inmagic yearly conference & regular meetings	Wish list evaluated, can do development at cost
Talis	Talis Alto	http://www.talis.com/products/product_select.shtml	–	Academic, Public	Regular	N	Via customer support	Via regular releases	Y	Via online forum, customer visits & annual conference. Evaluation of enhancement requests

*June 2005 – Sirsi and Dynix announce merger to form SirsiDynix (*http://www.sirsidynix.com/*).

This is where the importance of regular and rapid bug fixes plus customer influence on future development come in.

I have listed in Table 8.1 the main suppliers of Integrated Library Management Systems (ILMS) and stand-alone systems, as far as the UK is concerned, giving key information about their products. Note that this is not meant to be an exhaustive list. There is quite a range – from the small, UK and IDS-only supplier to global suppliers of complete systems. Each will have its advantages and disadvantages but in general they have similar ways of working. Ultimately, the question of which system is best will be answered on a case-by-case basis and will depend on the size and type of library it is to serve.

For some libraries the question will arise as to whether it is worth automating IDS as a whole. A library is likely to benefit from the automation of some IDS processes, such as sending a batch of requests to the British Library (BL), but it may be that the numbers of requests are too few to justify or require the purchase of a module or stand-alone system. This leads to the question of whether to go for an integrated or a stand-alone system, or possibly both. And what does the future hold regarding IDS generally – will it become part of Circulation or be incorporated into a new module of Direct Consortia Borrowing (DCB)?

To buy or not to buy?

Is an automated system really necessary? Before moving onto the procurement process it is worth examining whether an automated system for IDS is really required. There are plenty of libraries – school libraries for instance – that may have an automated system for general circulation traffic and cataloguing but do not need an IDS component. Below a certain level of IDS requests per year (several hundred?) it is questionable whether an IDS system is worth it – does the cost, maintenance and operation justify its existence, and is it really adding that much value? Even when the scale of IDS operation increases, the question is still valid as the IDS module will often be the weak link in a supplier's LMS. It is not unusual to find that the IDS module lags a long way behind other modules in terms of development and functionality. Furthermore, it is not unusual to find that certain important IDS functionality is missing – particularly with regards to working with systems at the British Library. This will be especially noticeable in systems that are new to the UK, where vendors are trying to break into a new market. If the functionality is not present, the development plan too long or the cost too high, these are all good reasons for sticking to manual-based systems or looking at a stand-alone. System suppliers are operating in a global marketplace and although there are many similarities between countries in terms of issuing and returning books, using MARC21 in cataloguing, checking in journal issues, etc., the unique way that UK interlending operates means that one system will not suit all. In the UK, interlending is largely dependent on the stock and services provided by the BL; outside the UK it is much more distributed. In the US, interlending relies heavily on consortia, as it does in Canada, although the National Library of Canada is involved as is CISTI, a major document supplier. The National Library of Australia plays a part in interlending for Australia but this is more as a support to a distributed network, and in Europe there is reliance on regional libraries and union catalogues. Even if libraries in these countries rely on the BL for their foreign requests it does not follow that IDS systems will therefore be suitable for UK libraries.

Procurement

Assuming you are still interested in buying a system, we can briefly look at the procurement process. By now some of the preliminary work will have been done – a need for a system will have been identified – and the next step is to look at what is available. This can be undertaken in an informal manner – researching the literature, finding out the main suppliers, seeing what is available, visiting exhibitions, talking to colleagues who have recently undergone the experience, etc. The budget you have available will give you a good idea of what you can get and from which suppliers. If you are in the public sector and the cost is above a certain figure (just under €250,000) then a tender advertisement in the Official Journal of the European Communities will be required. The tender will be based on a document that specifies the library's system requirements. This is called a Request For Proposal (RFP) and it describes in detail all the processes/functions that a system must have.

System suppliers will respond by ticking all the processes their system can supply, or identify work in progress and an estimated availability date. From this a short list can be drawn up and suppliers invited to demonstrate their systems on site. For major installations this will run over a number of days and allow library staff to gain hands-on experience. Staff should arrange visits to sites where the system is in place, to benefit from their knowledge and to see it working in a 'real' situation.

Once a decision is reached and a contract signed there begins the process of converting data, acquiring licences and, most likely, purchasing a lot of new hardware. Training will be provided by the supplier but library staff themselves will pass on training to colleagues. This will be undertaken during the implementation phase and will be an ongoing feature for the life of the system following upgrades and enhancements. Testing is another activity that will run and run. Large libraries will find a test server becomes an essential purchase, allowing them to install and test bug fixes and new versions before going live.

Once the system is 'live' the library is in the phase of ongoing support. This will include the reporting of bugs and the installation of fixes, requesting enhancements, networking with other users of the system, upgrading to new versions, plus acting as hosts to visitors from other libraries keen to see your shiny new library system.

The RFP is the most important and most time-consuming part of the process. It is also the most curious because it suggests that suppliers will be developing bespoke systems to suit their individual clients. What is really happening is that suppliers report on whether their existing systems perform the functions as outlined. Librarians spend considerable time detailing every last function that the system must be able to perform, or would like it to perform, and then suppliers spend considerable time (and money) responding to each item. Why is this? Well, partly it is because it is what is expected and how others have done it – libraries will share their RFP with others to copy, paste and adapt. Suppliers will tick off what their system can do. From personal experience I can say that every 'yes' from a supplier does not necessarily mean that the system can actually do what is asked. The main reason though is that this document will form the basis of the contract, and it will be much easier for the library if details are itemised and agreed, rather than discovering later that they are not available and so will require further expense to implement. Thankfully for all concerned there is a move towards standardising RFPs. Rather like a standard NESLI2 licence for acquiring and accessing e-journals that both publishers and librarians understand and find acceptable, a standard RFP is in development that suppliers and vendors can both utilise. OpenRFP is an American initiative which, as its website says, is where 'librarians meet their new software'.[2] A subset of this is the United Kingdom Core Specification (UKCS) which is where development work on the standard RFP is being undertaken.[3] This falls under the auspices of Juliet Leeves, a noted systems consultant.

Integrated or stand-alone?

Looking specifically at IDS, the advantages and disadvantages of integrated and stand-alone systems can be itemised (Table 8.2). It should be noted, however, that these are generalisations and so may not apply in specific cases.

For an IDS practitioner the stand-alone systems win out, offering better existing functionality, rapid development and a small community of dedicated users. However, the lack of integration with the main system that a library might have should not to be dismissed lightly. Development of the main system's IDS module together with questions over the long-term viability of the stand-alone product may decide the matter in favour of the ILMS. A compromise may be running two systems together – an ILMS for Circulation, Cataloguing, Serials, Acquisitions, etc., and a stand-alone for IDS. This can mean extra work and training but the benefits may be too great to resist. It explains why the Lancaster system – ILLOS – has done so well in the UK and is still in use in many libraries

Table 8.2   Comparison of integrated and stand-alone systems

Integrated		Stand-alone	
Advantages	Disadvantages	Advantages	Disadvantages
Links with other modules, e.g. Circulation – useful for user information, charges, placing stops, etc.	Development is slow and lags behind other modules	Development is quick, there are no other priority areas	No link to the ILMS, must keep own user data
	Existing functionality is poor to fair	Existing functionality is good to excellent	
Supplier is backed by significant resources	IDS is a minor part of the system	System is provided by a supplier specialising in IDS	Supplier does not have the resources of major systems suppliers
One system to work with and train on	Requires significant technical support to install and maintain	Requires little technical support to install and maintain	Other functions require another system

that otherwise run an ILMS. IS Oxford is an interesting example in that it is a relatively small company that has been operating successfully for some years. Its Heritage system has retained a large proportion of users who first bought it – in other words its customers are not moving to other systems. Yet Heritage IV does not, and has never, offered an IDS component – only now (spring–summer 2005) is development on an IDS module underway. This begs a number of interesting questions, such as why it has taken so long, what have libraries been using for IDS, etc.? The reason for lack of demand from customers, and therefore lack of development, has been because libraries are using other products, typically the WinCHILL stand-alone system. So libraries can run more than one system to manage their day-to-day transactions. Of course, an alternative is to produce your own in-house system, as the University of Manchester has done. But this may be taking things too far.

Typically, stand-alone systems are small, simple to install and maintain, easy to manage, provide up-to-date functionality and can develop rapidly. WinCHILL and ILLOS are specific to the UK but ILL Manager is a product developed by the American Research Libraries Group (RLG). ILL is being used by a small number of higher education libraries which are part of the SHARES international interlending programme as a means of requesting material, as it offers ISO-ILL and SHARES compatibility. These libraries are using it in conjunction with other ILMS that do not yet offer ISO-ILL and SHARES functionality. It remains to be seen whether they will continue to use ILL Manager once the main system is up to speed.

Alternatives

I questioned earlier whether buying a whole system, or an IDS module, was really necessary. This question is likely to be particularly pertinent for smaller libraries. The cost of purchasing a system, the hardware on which to run it and the staff to maintain and update it may simply be prohibitive. Or perhaps there are no or too few staff with the necessary IT skills. For those libraries still wanting an automated system, but lacking the resources to run one, there is another option: the ASP. The ASP, Application Service Provider, is where a supplier hosts the software and any supporting applications, such as Oracle, while offering functionality through a 'thin client' or via the Web. The customer library therefore has very little to do in the way of installation, maintenance or upgrades. Typically, ASP versions of systems are provided on a subscription basis.

One supplier remarked to me that prospective ASP customers will be very concerned with security, and will typically want as standard something far in advance of anything they would have if they themselves were hosting the system. As a leader in the field, Softlink hold their applications deep underground in Chicago in an environment that would not look out of place in a Mission Impossible film:

> Access to the data centre is limited to select host employees. To access the secure cage housing our equipment, one must pass through two guard stations (staffed 24 hours a day, 365 days a year), and five locked doors. Biometric scanners protect every door. The entire facility is covered by video surveillance, with tapes retained for 30 days.[4]

Not only are security fears placated but library staff can be reassured that should a disaster strike then essential data will not be destroyed by fire or flood. An ASP version of a system can therefore be an attractive proposition on a number of fronts.

Continuing with the security issue, and thinking about systems in general, you may want to think about possible disasters beyond everyday threats of fire, flood, locusts and hackers. Examples can be the sudden financial collapse or takeover of the supplier. To insure against such disasters and ensure business continuity, suppliers and libraries can make use of software escrow accounts with specialist companies. A typical arrangement will see a supplier paying to deposit the software source code with such a company, while a customer pays an annual subscription that entitles it to use that source code if ever an agreed 'trigger event' occurs, e.g. supplier insolvency. Although this level of security can bring peace of mind, many may find it excessive.

An alternative to the standard system is one based on Open Source software. We have talked about depositing source code in an escrow account and how this can be released to those contracted to do so. Open Source is a movement that encourages programmers and developers to make source code freely available. Others are then free to use this source code to produce systems and develop it further. The movement, which is what Open Source essentially is, has grown rapidly since its inception in 1998. The Linux operating system is perhaps the most well-known example of Open Source software, but there are many other products, such as the Microsoft Office alternative, OpenOffice, that are used around the world today. CyberLibrary is a company that markets an Open Source LMS in the UK, but although it claims to cover all aspects of library management there is no mention of IDS. A specifically IDS system that is Open Source-based is that produced by the University of Winnipeg and partners, OpenILL. Its origin can be traced back to 2002 when a high level of dissatisfaction with existing commercial IDS systems prompted action from several individuals. It is currently run as a co-operative project involving Canadian university libraries and is priced according to the level of commitment that institutions are prepared to make. OpenILL shows what can be done if you do not like existing options: build your own. It also shows that just because a product is Open Source that does not mean it cannot be sold. The source code is always freely available but the product that is developed from that code can command a price.

What to do with the system once you have got it

Ideally the system should do exactly what you want it to and be flexible enough to accommodate changes in procedure. Realistically, however, library staff can find themselves having to adapt procedures or policy to fit with what the system can handle. This is not necessarily a bad thing. Being forced into making changes can be a kick-start to the imagination and result in improved ways of working. What might at first be labelled a 'bug', because it does not allow staff to work in a way they have been used to, can turn into a preferred way of working, so that even if the 'bug' is fixed staff do not return to former practices.

Strictly speaking the problem as outlined above should not be termed a 'bug'; rather it is more of an enhancement or development request. A bug is where the system is not working at it is supposed to. Generally, bugs and enhancements are easy to distinguish, but grey areas do exist. What if something works in one version but no longer works in the new version – does that count as a bug? Does any of this matter, or is it just an example of librarians being overly concerned with classification again? Well, yes it does matter because a supplier will set about fixing a bug in the short term, whereas an enhancement enjoys a more perilous existence – it may not actually make it into the product – and is in any case more of a mid-term solution. Being prepared to argue your case for a problem to be classified as a bug can pay dividends.

It should be easy to report bugs, and, as can be seen from Table 8.1, each of the suppliers listed has a simple means of doing so – phone, email, Web – and a support unit to handle them. Suppliers may need to replicate the problem, in which case they may require remote access to servers and an example to work on. Fixes should be quick and will entail the supplier fixing remotely or releasing a 'patch' to install. The most serious cases will mean that parts or all of the system are unavailable, and may see the reintroduction of paper forms and the typing of long lists of requests as email to BLDSC; less serious problems can be overcome by a workaround until a fix is implemented.

A manual on system/module use should be created if one is not available from the supplier. Local modifications should be documented.

Future development

The main driving force behind system development is the requirements of new customers. Breaking into a new market – country, sector – or targeting prestige institutions will inevitably necessitate fast-track development to secure sales. What these customers want before they sign they will get. This can be a route for existing customers to push their development requests, if they have been in contact with potential new customers. Existing customers may well be astonished at the speed of progress in development if an attractive customer is to be snared. For existing customers the stairway to functionality heaven can be long and arduous.

The existence of a user group can act as a channel or lobbying body for enhancements, as well as providing a conduit for communication with the supplier, dealing with complaints, news, demonstrations of new products, etc. How influential and useful these groups are varies considerably, depending on the supplier's view of the relationship and the commitment of members, as it will fall to interested individuals to keep the group active. Whether IDS exists as a group on its own or as part of a larger group will also play a part in its success or otherwise. It is important for IDS practitioners themselves to be active participants in any user group because their needs can be overlooked. This applies to any practitioners, as user groups are often made up of systems librarians. And systems are too important to be left to systems librarians.

Although the systems suppliers detailed in Table 8.1. report that they bring out updated versions fairly regularly (at least once a year), it should be remembered that development work in ILMS will vary from module to module. The new version might be little different from the previous version.

Typically, enhancement requests go through some sort of evaluation procedure. Suppliers will look at the requests, and assess their usefulness and how much work it will take to implement them. The assessment of usefulness may largely be left to customers to decide through voting, with the most popular making it into the system. This can be a major disadvantage if IDS is part of an ILMS and the ILMS is treated as a whole for the voting, as IDS will inevitably rate low in the hierarchy. If it then has to compete against requests from other countries, it will suffer further, owing to the special nature of UK interlending, as mentioned above. What then becomes essential is the willingness of the supplier to commit to developing the product in collaboration with customers, outside of any formal voting process. If the supplier is prepared to work closely with existing customers to develop the product that can only be to their mutual advantage. The supplier will produce a superior product and the customers will strengthen their commitment to it, influencing others.

Interlending beyond the IDS module

A recent trend in interlending is the move to 'patron-initiated requesting' or DCB. This has taken off in the US and in all likelihood will come to the UK in some form. Essentially it removes the IDS intermediary, placing the 'locate and request' processes in the hands of users who interact directly with other libraries. A user searches a union catalogue, finds the item he or she wants and then reserves or requests it. The library holding the item then sends it to the user's preferred library or perhaps directly to the user. Transactions are handled by circulation staff, rather than IDS staff. Such schemes that have been set up are all based on consortia; there is the need for a union catalogue and agreement on who can request (their rights and responsibilities), etc. Although existing consortia provide a ready-made market for this type of interlending, there is nothing to stop non-consortia libraries from linking up with interested partners. So far these schemes have reported much faster turnaround times and significant cost savings.

Rather than simply allowing circulation modules to handle these requests, systems suppliers have been developing consortia borrowing modules – either as separate entities or as part of IDS. Based on the NISO Circulation Interchange Protocol, and incorporating the DCB application, these modules can then be sold to libraries that are not existing customers because they are not dependent on using the supplier's main LMS. Dynix and Innovative Interfaces are two companies marketing DCB applications in addition to traditional LMS.

In the UK it is hoped that COPAC will be developed to incorporate some IDS functionality, perhaps leading to unmediated requesting and delivery.

A few words on the suppliers

Now that we have looked at systems generally it is worth looking more closely at the suppliers and their systems as itemised in Table 8.1. Although I do not want to go into detail about how each system handles IDS transactions, I nevertheless think some useful points can be made. As already mentioned, the range of suppliers is considerable. Clio Software, for example, is a small, family-run business, originally from New Hampshire. Its website lists the individual family members and where they are based, and now one non-family member, and where he is based, involved in producing Clio IDS. It seems to hark back to an earlier time of craftsmen hand-producing quality goods. What is also interesting is that Clio Software not only produces its own IDS system, but also provides the module for Endeavor's Voyager system. Here then is an example of a system that comes directly from those working in IDS and one that has been tailored to fit into a larger integrated system from a different supplier.

Related to this was the news that Sirsi was to market the Relais ILL client in the UK. Relais International is a company based in Ottawa that is best known in the UK for producing scanning and delivery systems for the BL. It has its own IDS stand-alone system, Relais ILL, which was to be sold in the UK through Sirsi. This news, however, came before the announcement of Sirsi's merger with Dynix, and the commitment to continuing with both companies' systems – Unicorn, Corinthian, Horizon as well as the URSA application. Although support for these products must continue for a few years, I would not expect the company to continue with such a range for long. In all likelihood, Relais ILL will be incorporated into Unicorn or into any product that SirsiDynix offers with IDS functionality.

Another company that provides systems for the BL is Fretwell Downing Informatics (FDI). FDI is rather unusual, and I would think unique, in that its IDS product – VDX – is probably better known, at least in the UK, than its LMS – OLIB7. VDX is the software that underpins the BL's ISO gateway. It has been widely used in Australia and is being used by the public library partnership, Co-East, in the UK to facilitate interlending. Public libraries in The Netherlands are also using VDX to provide a joined-up national network for their users.

Many of the suppliers are quite small in size and contrast quite strongly with the 'juggernauts', as one supplier labelled them to me in an interview. A difference that is particularly noticeable is the attitude to marketing and sales. Clio Software have the following on their website:

> We don't have an army of marketing or sales people, so you won't be getting any high-pressure sales calls or visits from us.

A similar approach is adopted by IS Oxford who stress that they 'try to avoid the traditional mentality associated with the sales lifestyle', and seem more concerned with retaining existing customers and keeping them happy rather than relentlessly pursuing new ones. This seems refreshingly different from what one would expect in a very competitive market.

I have already mentioned IS Oxford's lack of an IDS module in an otherwise 'complete' system, but it is also interesting to note how those suppliers who do have an IDS module sometimes seem to try and hide the fact. Take a look at Geac's website as an example: while there are descriptions of their various systems there is no mention of IDS or something similar. To be fair, Geac is in a process of transition from Advance to Vubis Smart but this is probably the worst case I have come across. However, there are quite a few suppliers who do not deem it necessary to highlight that their system has an IDS component.

Another striking difference is that whereas the 'juggernauts' will try and produce a universal system, the smaller suppliers may well have different systems for different markets and even different versions of the same system. Softlink is perhaps best known for its Alice system, most often used in school libraries, but although there are four different versions of Alice, none of them incorporates IDS. Liberty3, which does have IDS, has been produced for the corporate and special libraries market, and Oliver is an alternative to Alice in the education market. Bailey Solutions have four LMS products with two of them incorporating IDS functionality. Particularly in a global market, having one system to suit all can lead to a very complex product. There will be competing claims for enhancements while customers will also want to ensure that existing functionality is not lost.

The importance of development has already been stressed. Again it can be considerably easier to influence development and a lot quicker to see results from smaller suppliers. Being able to report directly to suppliers what you would like to see in a later version, and having a realistic expectation that such wishes will soon be part and parcel of a system, is a terrific boon to customers. A number of suppliers reported to me that what customers say they would like to see as enhancements are often already in the pipeline for development. A few suppliers offer to undertake development either at cost or partial cost to the customer, depending on how 'utilitarian' the requested development is likely to prove.

As can be seen, the relationship between a library and its system supplier is crucial. A poor working relationship will prompt an earlier than expected look for alternatives. But even if the rapport is good it is still good practice to re-evaluate what the market has to offer. A review at least every 10 years should be the minimum.

Thanks

Thanks to the various systems suppliers mentioned for providing information on their products.

Notes

1. Myhill, Martin (2000) 'Time for change. A personal insight into library systems' implementation: experiences at Exeter University library', *Program* 34(1): 89–101.
2. OpenRFP: *http://www.openrfi.com/cfm/si_pd.cfm?*
3. OpenRFP UK Core Specification: *http://www.openrfi.com/cfm/si_pd.cfm? PID=12*
4. Softlink Europe (2004) *Softlink ASP Hosting Infrastructure*. Promotional literature.

9

Delivery in interlending and document supply

Stephen Prowse

The most important part of interlending and document supply (IDS) is delivery – getting the requested item into the hands of the requester. Everything else is just processing. However, when we look at the various formats that are being delivered we are faced with quite a stark difference. Items that are available electronically – whether born-digital or made-digital – can be delivered extremely quickly and efficiently, whereas those that are non-electronic are subject to delay, loss or damage, and high delivery costs. And it is journal articles that are most likely to be available, or made available, electronically. But even if articles are copied to paper they are still more easily supplied than loans. Such factors can ultimately affect decisions on whether actually to lend items to other libraries. The negative impact is most particularly felt when it comes to international supply.

Discovery is another area that shows up major differences. Publishers and aggregators provide interfaces to electronic journals, and link resolvers allow users to navigate to full text or other services easily and quickly. A national union catalogue for serials, SUNCAT, is in the process of being rolled out whereas an attempt at a national union catalogue for monographs has stalled.

In this chapter I shall be looking at various means of delivery and how developments in technology, such as link resolvers, provide almost effortless search and retrieval. However, just in case things appear to be all too easy, it should be noted that the electronic world brings with it a number of its own restrictions, and I shall be looking at those too.

Discover, locate, request

The huge growth of the Internet has meant that many tools of discovery are now easily available to everyone. Library catalogues, including union catalogues, for major national, public, academic and special libraries across the world can now be accessed online. Web pages provide indexes to the different types. Certain catalogues, such as COPAC, provide real-time circulation information whereas others provide a requesting mechanism once an item has been found. We saw in the previous chapter how consortia are using their union catalogues as a mechanism for IDS, utilising the Direct Consortia Borrowing applications. In such an environment, interlending becomes circulation. The British Library's (BL) Integrated Catalogue brings together a number of its important catalogues, providing information on over 12 million items. Items can be requested via the Catalogue – copies for anyone, loans and copies for registered customers. As the Catalogue does not cover the vast stock of the BL, items may also be requested if they are not found.

I discuss link resolvers in the next section. Although they are useful for discovering items they achieve their peak of usefulness in taking users to the full text.

So, for a wide range of material it has become relatively easy to trace a location. However, this is only the beginning, as now there is the question of getting hold of the actual item. This too though has, by and large, become considerably easier. Nevertheless, there is significant progress still to be made in a number of areas.

Delivery

About 80% of the items supplied by the BL are copies, as opposed to loans. And around 20% of those are supplied electronically. It used to be that the BL housed a large number of photocopiers to supply paper copies, but today these have been replaced by scanners. This change took place over a relatively short period and it is interesting to see how it came about. As the BL is the major supplier of journal articles, such examination will also provide an opportunity to look at how the delivery of copies has developed generally.

In the United States, libraries have enjoyed a longer history of supplying and receiving articles electronically thanks to the Ariel software developed by the Research Libraries Group (RLG). This was first launched in DOS format in 1990 as a much better alternative to the fax. A Windows version was released in 1994 and has grown to become the standard software for transmitting articles across the Internet. Items are scanned as Tiff images, which can be sent via ftp or email to other PCs running Ariel, or directly to users. The Tiff files can be converted into PDF if preferred and passed on by libraries to users by email or printed out for them to collect. The idea behind Ariel was that libraries could purchase cheap software that would not require a lot of extra, expensive equipment to run it. This software could then be used to supply and receive good quality copies, at a faster and cheaper rate than fax would provide.

It is worth noting at this point that libraries in the US have been supplying documents directly by electronic means to users since the late 1990s. There has not been the paranoia about infringing copyright that has hampered development of such services in the UK. To facilitate patron delivery some software was written and developed by staff at the Prior Health Sciences Library at Ohio State University that could be used in conjunction with Ariel. Named 'Prospero' to provide a *Tempest* tie-in with Ariel, the software manages the processes of delivering the article to the user. Prospero provides for the creation of a simple patron database with email addresses for notification, conversion of Tiff files to PDF, and enables delivery of the article either directly by email or to a server for a user to collect, and removal from the server a number of days later. Such has been its usefulness and success that the functionality was incorporated into version 3 of Ariel.

It was only with the launch of LAMDA in 1995 that UK use of Ariel started to take off. This was initially an e-Lib project involving higher education (HE) libraries in London and Manchester, set up to act as suppliers of journal articles to each other and to other customer libraries. Ariel was the means of delivery. As LAMDA began life as a project, funding was available to provide customer libraries within HE with free copies of Ariel. Once a number of UK libraries started using Ariel, the BL began offering to supply by this means too. It had been supplying US libraries but until LAMDA there was no market for Ariel supply in the UK. It should be remembered that the BL saw LAMDA libraries as competitors and so wanted to match whatever service was being offered.

Ariel continues to be used but there must be a question mark over its future in the UK. In 2003 RLG sold Ariel to Infotrieve, a US-based information supplier. When version 4 was launched in 2004 it was accompanied by the announcement that it would not be compatible with versions earlier than 3. As version 2 was the version that had been distributed free this would have posed a dilemma to those libraries that had not upgraded to 3. There was also a compatibility problem with ILL Manager. Thankfully, both these problems have been overcome, but this has not been a good pointer to future development. Since the release of version 3 a free version is no longer available to HE libraries and Ariel itself has become quite expensive. More importantly though, there are two developments which will have a negative impact on Ariel: (1) the BL has introduced a Secure Electronic Delivery (SED) service which it is keen to establish as the primary mechanism for supplying electronic copies, and (2) LAMDA folded at the end of July 2005. It remains to be seen if there are other avenues open to Ariel use such as in document supply from co-operative stores of low-use material, but, if not, then its use is likely to decline.

Primarily aimed at the commercial sector, the BL's Inside service became Web-based in 1997. Initially launched in 1991, Inside is a service built on a database of the top 20,000 journals plus conference papers requested from the BL. Users, or library staff on their behalf, can search for papers or scan journal contents pages and request delivery of selected articles. A budget can be set and managed by library staff but users can then be left to buy articles for themselves. As such, it became an attractive proposition for the wealthy commercial sector. Increasingly, articles have become electronically available for immediate download and this expansion of provision continues apace.

A service introduced in 2005 with similarities to Inside is BL Direct. This is for journal articles only and is aimed at individual researchers rather than intermediaries. The main difference from Inside lies in the lack of management tools that an IDS manager would need. Based on a smaller database – only covering the last 5 years – BL Direct offers SED delivery and instant download as well as mail. In its drive to promote its services directly to users, the BL will be pushing BL Direct as a gateway to document supply. It will run in parallel with Inside.

The availability of articles for immediate download or by SED has only come about thanks to the solution to the digital rights management (DRM) problem. But before describing this solution we should look at what gave rise to the problem in the first place, and, of course, describe what precisely was the problem.

e-Journals – the problem of being

The rise in supplying documents electronically has coincided with the growth of electronic journals. At first, online availability was limited to recent years but we have seen publishers digitising their backfiles and making these available in packages for purchase. Additionally, e-journals are often marketed and sold as bundles or 'Big Deals' – a publisher's whole journal output available in one package for example. Not surprisingly, the rise in ready access to e-journals has led to a drop in demand for articles via IDS. But if a library has increased access to scholarly output for its own users, it may not be able to help out other libraries requesting articles for their users. In the print world, libraries can copy and deliver (electronically if they have the means) articles to other libraries from their own stock, within the constraints of copyright law. In the electronic world, these constraints become far more restrictive.

Firstly, libraries do not own e-journals like they do print journals. Ownership is more in the form of a leasing arrangement. A subscription will entitle electronic access to a title for the years that the subscription is valid. Once cancelled there may be continued access, as outlined in the licence agreement, but equally there may well be loss of access to previously available content. Although post-termination access is now quite common, it is not always the case. There are a number of deals where a subscription will provide access to current and back content which will both be lost once the subscription ends. Even where archival access is guaranteed there remains the question of how this access will be maintained. Access may continue through the publisher's online interface if the library remains a customer for other titles or pays an annual maintenance charge. Alternatively the content is made available to libraries in other formats.

The fact that libraries are now less likely to lose access after cancelling subscriptions is largely thanks to agreements reached in the National Electronic Site Licensing Initiatives – PSLI, NESLI and NESLI2. The Negotiation Agent, Content Complete, meets with a number of publishers with a view to securing beneficial terms for an annual (or sometimes longer) deal for HE and FE institutions. The list of publishers is drawn from a selection recommended by representatives in HE and FE libraries. There will be a main list of about 10 publishers and a reserve list of about three, should any of the first 10 not be able to agree terms. What the negotiations are based on is a previously agreed 'model' licence. This covers all the important areas of access to e-journals – terms of use, post-termination access, walk-in use and document delivery. In the offers that go out to the HE and FE communities publishers will state where they comply with or differ from the model licence. It is now more common for publishers to permit document delivery of articles from e-journals to other libraries. However, achieving this has been a long struggle and the reason why it has taken so long lies in the difference between electronic and print.

In the electronic world items can be made available to a wide audience very quickly. The print world can reach the same audience but only after taking much longer and with greater effort. If an article can be widely distributed in an instant then there is the fear that licence restrictions will be broken. A user can download an article from an e-journal and email it to colleagues who do not have access to it via their institutions, and who have not paid to obtain it via document delivery. As a result, publishers lose revenue. We have seen the same concerns in the entertainment industry – illegal downloads of music driving down legitimate sales, pirate copies of films hitting profits. To combat these problems a twin approach has been adopted – prosecution and closure of websites, and encryption built into materials, such as CDs, and hardware, such as DVD players. It is only more recently that we have seen agreements reached with record companies and the establishment of services offering music downloads at a price or subscription. Encryption can be considered part of DRM, ensuring that only 'authorised' users can access the content. However, the quest for protecting assets can have unfortunate side-effects such as CDs not playing on PCs. The latest version of Microsoft Office makes much of facilitating the sharing of documents and information with colleagues while managing what they are able to do with them. As in all questions involving copyright it is ultimately a question of balance – between the rights of users and those of rights holders. Users who infringe the rights of rights holders will often point to the high cost of content, particularly in 'rip-off Britain', as a justification. If we have to pay a lot more to obtain our music than those in Europe or the US then there is little sympathy for the plight of record companies. Journal publishers, too, are long used to complaints about the costs of their products, although that has not stopped them milking the market for what it is worth.

In order to be able to supply journal articles by electronic means, the BL has had to reach agreement with publishers and allay their fears over potential abuse once the copy is in the hands of the user. If an article is supplied via Ariel then libraries must have agreed not to tamper with the format, e.g. changing Tiff to PDF. But for wider application something else was needed. This has turned out to be the Adobe Content Server and Reader. Using the DRM capabilities of Adobe products the BL has been able to set up an SED service. In SED the BL will scan an article, encrypt it and load it as a PDF onto a server. An email will be sent to the user or an intermediary giving notice of availability and the URL. The user can then print or download the article. What the user will not be able to do is print additional copies or forward it to other users electronically. The built-in DRM component will ensure that restrictions are enforced. These vary according to whether the article has been ordered via the Library Privilege service, but there will be a time restriction on how long the article resides on the server. Since the BL replaced its photocopiers with scanners all articles are now processed by scanning, even if being sent out on paper by post. The same DRM functionality is used in supplying articles via the Inside service. If an agreement has been reached with a publisher then an article may be available for immediate download. Otherwise it can be made available electronically and delivered via SED. Thanks to the protection offered by DRM in Adobe more publishers are willing to permit their content to be made instantly available via Inside. They are also happy to see articles delivered by SED. From 1 August 2005, delivery by SED or Ariel became cheaper than by post. Keen to encourage customers to move to electronic delivery, this is the first time that the BL has offered a financial incentive to do so.

Engaging publishers

IDS has always been a somewhat problematic area for journal publishers. There has long been a concern that the supply of articles by the BL was being used as a substitute for subscriptions. Research has shown that this is not the case, but concerns remain. The rise of e-journals has brought the fear of revenue loss to document delivery in a wider sense. Publishers have sought and imposed restrictions on use in a number of areas such as no document delivery permitted, or document delivery only if numerous data are collected – who, what, when. Restricting to single sites of multi-site institutions, or placing limits on workstations or users, e.g. walk-in use, or number of concurrent users, are other examples. These restrictions, however, are easing as publishers become more reassured about how their content is being used. Many publishers of course offer their own 'pay as you go' document delivery service, providing articles to users who pay by credit card. But, apart from the BL, publisher collaboration with libraries in the field of IDS has not been a great success. The experience of two fledgling document delivery services will demonstrate this point.

EASY (Electronic Article SupplY) was an interesting collaboration between the e-journals aggregator, ingenta, and Lancaster University, developer of the IDS management system ILLOS. It was developed as a possible solution to the document delivery dilemma as outlined above. In EASY, publishers would receive some payment from document delivery, which they do not receive in conventional IDS. They would also obtain valuable information on use of their content. For librarians, their users would have access to online articles if they were available, or paper copies via IDS if they were not – all from a single service. Furthermore, any articles delivered via ingenta would not be charged at a higher cost than traditional IDS, and users would not have to sign copyright declarations, although they would of course be bound by the terms and conditions of the service. Nineteen publishers, including Kluwer Academic and Oxford University Press, agreed to participate in EASY. The project ran from 1 March 2001 to 30 June 2002. In the first phase it was restricted to users of the ILLOS library management system (LMS) but the idea was that if this proved successful EASY would expand to users of other LMS. Unfortunately, just as this expansion had started the project folded. One problem was the limited coverage – as is well-known in IDS there are relatively few journals that generate a lot of requests of articles but an inordinate number that generate only one or two requests each. Many of the publishers involved were fairly small concerns who could not hope to provide a critical mass of articles. Another problem lay in the matching of article titles in the requests to the articles themselves – this had to be close to an exact match even though 'fuzzy' matching had been adopted. Although these were undoubtedly major obstacles, the more serious problem was the lack of engagement from publishers, who felt it was not in their interest to participate. If publishers have set up their own article supply business why should they link up with someone else doing the same thing? Co-operating with the BL is one thing but joining with much smaller services holds no appeal. In the end only 139 requests had been filled via EASY.[1]

Eventually it was hoped that EASY would link up with another project that was getting started at around the same time. Docusend was planned to be a document delivery service that would build on LAMDA but, like EASY, would also include a number of publishers as partners. Unlike LAMDA, the BL would also be involved. The LAMDA libraries would act as article suppliers, as would the BL, but again it was hoped that publishers could deliver PDF versions of their articles. The trials and tribulations of Docusend have been well documented.[2] It suffered its share of technical difficulties but in a sense it was a project that was overtaken by advances elsewhere. The rapid development of link resolvers, such as SFX, enabled users to be taken directly to full text rather than having to proceed via a service such as Docusend. The other key factor was that no publisher agreed to act as a supplier. But then there was little incentive for them to do so.

Link resolvers

A link resolver will take you from a bibliographic record such as a citation in a database to a list of services for that item and then onwards. The most useful service will typically be a link to the full text itself, but if the library does not subscribe to the journal in which the article appears then other options are available, such as a link to the abstract, to the table of contents for that issue, the offer to conduct a search in a library catalogue or a search engine such as Google, or to request the item via IDS. Next to each item found in a search a button will be presented to users to click for a menu of services. How the resolver works is based on two important components – the OpenURL and a database of resources.

The OpenURL is a standard permitting interoperability between a piece of metadata and services for that metadata, as in the situation above. It comprises two parts – a URL, pointing to the resolver of the user's library, and a Query, comprising the metadata for the item. Here is an example:

http://sfx.kcl.ac.uk:9003/kings?genre=article&issn=00330337& date=2000&volume=34&issue=1&spage=75&epage=87&aulast= prowse&__char_set=utf8

The metadata contains a number of common elements; in this case we have: the type of item (article), ISSN, date, volume and issue numbers, the first and last pages, and the author's last name. Pointing to the location of the user's resolver will therefore show only 'appropriate' services for that user, e.g. only a full text link will be shown where the user is entitled to access the full text. Publishers make their resources OpenURL-compliant. Once publishers and providers have been informed of the URL of a library's resolver, linking can take place.

The database of resources will be provided and regularly updated by the supplier of the resolver. It will contain collections of e-journals and other resources that library staff can then activate where a subscription is in place. This activation can be for the whole package, for selected titles within a package and for selected years only. Therefore, library staff have control over which resources can be accessed as well control over what services are offered.

The beauty of link resolvers for users is that much of the work of locating and accessing material is eliminated. Users no longer have to take the reference for a journal article, look the journal up in a library's catalogue or A–Z Web page and then go and retrieve the item – a few clicks and they can be reading it.

Digital object identifiers (DOIs) are another way of gaining access to resources. Unlike URLs, which can change, a DOI is a permanent tag to an item, such as a journal article. It is a string of alphanumeric characters that uniquely identify an item, e.g. 10.1300/J110v10n02_05. Like the Open URL it is made up of two parts – the prefix identifies the publisher or authority and the suffix identifies the particular item. In this case we have the following elements: the journal (represented as J110), volume (v10), issue (n02) and the number of the article in that issue (05). The DOI can be presented as a link or it can be typed into the DOI resolver (available at *http://dx.doi.org/*). DOIs are managed by the International DOI Foundation via a number of Registration Agencies (RA) who allocate the prefixes and register the DOIs. CrossRef, for example, is a well-known RA formed by the world's leading scholarly publishers. As well as providing a unique, permanent identifier, the DOI can function as a link, taking users to the full text. However, users will not reach the full text if their library does not subscribe to the material. In this respect the DOI is not a substitute for the Open URL, it is more likely to form part of one.

Loans

The overwhelming majority of monographs loaned by the BL each year are to academic libraries. The system has worked well for many years but questions have been asked of its ongoing suitability. There are a number of problem areas with monograph interlending. Declining investment in stock, the loan of old or rare stock, and the cost of loans from the BL are some examples. Transporting books between libraries is also a problem which preoccupies many IDS staff.

For many years, the BL and the regional library systems worked together to run van services to transport material around the UK. The end of the various schemes in 1999 saw the break-up of reliable, cheap and efficient services. The vacuum was largely filled by Royal Mail and a company called HaysDX. Sadly, for many IDS staff, HaysDX has been a disaster, responsible for too many lost or damaged books. A number of libraries started insisting that the company was not used to return their stock. In late 2004 HaysDX split, with DX becoming responsible for the transport and delivery of mail. Some libraries use other courier services instead, or Parcel Force. The BL uses a combination of courier services and the Royal Mail. There may be further changes in the near future, as Royal Mail has plans to change its pricing policy. From 2006 parcels will be charged according to size rather than weight.

Loans sent directly to users

The BL's AddAddress service allows IDS staff to decide whether a request is to be sent to the library or direct to the end user. In practice this usually means photocopies rather than loans, owing to fears of loss or damage in transit. (A lost book from the BL costs well over £100 to replace.) However, it does give library staff the option to have a book sent direct to a reader who is unable to come into the library to collect a loan.

The growth of distance learning has encouraged libraries to provide postal loans to students, but few IDS or consortial services send books direct to readers. Innovative interlending schemes such as Linc y Gogledd still require users to go to a collection point. The use of Direct Consortial Borrowing has been a hit in the US but has made no impact in the UK. Yet the advent of unmediated requesting and delivery cannot be too far away. It has happened with copies and it will happen with monographs. Although a place for traditional IDS will remain, services aimed at reducing or eliminating the role of the intermediary will be the future.

Notes

1. Thanks to Andy Hartland of Lancaster University for information on EASY.
2. Bower, Gordon (2005) 'Docusend: the one-stop, integrated, document delivery broker service', *Interlending and Document Supply* 33(1): 8–13; Bell, Anne; Bower, Gordon; Whitehurst, David (2004) 'Docusend: the one-stop, integrated, document delivery broker service – final report', available at *http://www.docusend.ac.uk/final.pdf*

10

The interlending and document supply department

Neil Dalley and Tracey Jackson

IDS in the library structure

The interlending and document supply (IDS) department may be large enough to operate as a distinct and separate section within the library structure but it is more common for it to be a subsection of other library operations. It may be managed as a part of the overall circulation or reader services offered by the library or it may be seen as a bibliographic service and run alongside acquisition and cataloguing functions. The latter model appears to be most common in public libraries, but greater variety exists in the academic sector. The independence of IDS from its parent section will depend very much on the size of the operation and the type, and seniority, of staff in place.

Both models have their advantages. A circulation-based section should focus on readers and services, whereas a section within bibliographic services has the advantage of being able to complement acquisition decisions. In many public libraries, a book requested by a reader is normally purchased; only if it is too expensive or too esoteric for the library to buy, or is out-of-print, is it referred to IDS. Liaison between acquisition and interlending decisions should perhaps be more routine in other sorts of libraries as well.

The physical location of the department is also significant. In some institutions IDS staff are available at a desk to answer queries directly from readers, whereas in others they only communicate with readers through other front-line staff or by phone, email, etc. An IDS information point has the advantage of raising the department's profile and allowing you to develop a relationship with your readers. It does, however, involve more staff time and can detract from the processing side of the work. As online requesting becomes more prevalent the role of a specific public contact point is perhaps less significant.

Staffing

Staffing levels

Depending on the structure of the department, staff may undertake IDS duties alongside the other tasks the larger section has to fulfil, or they may devote most of their time to IDS work. In almost all institutions staff will have to contribute to other library tasks such as shelving or front-line services. This makes any calculation of the staffing needed for a section very difficult. In most libraries staffing levels have arisen out of past experience, and will reflect the number of requests received and the amount of hands-on work done on requests or value-added services offered.

From an informal survey carried out among 34 lis-ill members in 2005 we saw that the total number of both incoming and outgoing requests varied enormously. Some institutions dealt with a few hundred a year whereas others received over 30,000. Comparing the ratio of staff to requests received we saw that there was a huge variation, which must be due in part to the amount of time staff devote to non-IDS tasks. In one institution each member of staff (full-time equivalent) would have dealt with only 460 requests if they were shared equally among them throughout the year, whereas in another each staff member would have dealt with 7000 requests. On average, each staff member dealt with 2960 requests in the course of the year. Although this clearly is not a scientifically accurate figure it certainly gives some indication of the number of staff required. It is worth noting that dealing with requests from other libraries tends to be more time-consuming than ordering documents for your own readers. Retrieving material from distant shelves and copying articles are both labour-intensive tasks.

Types of staff

It is good to have staff who specialise in IDS, even if they do other jobs as well. They will quickly build up expertise in the area, which will enhance the speed and quality of the service you offer. People who know about IDS and are proud of the service are vital if you want the section to thrive. Ideally assistants will have some previous library experience, because of the way the work interconnects with that of other sections. Perhaps more important is an ability to see the work they are doing from the users' perspective, and so customer-service experience is invaluable.

We would argue for a head of the section who has a clear responsibility for developing the area and is able to build up their own expertise and knowledge. Some libraries choose to employ a professional librarian in this role, but this will depend on the organisation's priorities and attitudes towards professional qualifications. Our survey in 2005 suggested that professional staff involvement is more common in academic and research libraries than in the public library sector, and just under half the responding institutions had staff with a professional qualification involved in the section.

Formal qualifications are not vital, but what is essential is that the head of section is given sufficient influence and power to drive forward change in the department and to investigate and develop the use of new technology and new services. IDS is proving to be a rapidly changing area and the service must not fossilise. The head of section should monitor what other institutions are doing, and have the authority to make policy decisions (or at least recommendations) based on their findings about new developments.

In many cases the head of section will not be involved in the day-to-day processing within the department, and so be able to concentrate on service development. In a smaller organisation he or she might combine this role with another function. In many cases, those closer to the routine work will find it easier to evaluate and judge new services. Alternatively, service development may be the responsibility of higher management. In this case sufficient time must be allowed for IDS alongside other responsibilities.

Staff training

Staff are the most valuable (and most expensive) asset the IDS department has, so it is vitally important that time and energy is invested in their training.

When new staff begin work in the section it is advisable to give them some background information about how IDS fits in with the overall aims and objectives of your institution and your library service. You should also explain how the section relates to the other services your library offers. It will be valuable if you can discuss the way the IDS process works on a national basis. Make sure that all staff who work in the section understand the importance of co-operation with other institutions. Libraries have to be willing to help each other.

As well as practical training on your own Library Management System (LMS) and the practical routines their job involves, you should also consider training in the following areas:

- How to check references against your own catalogue and the most effective searching techniques.
- Bibliographic references and how to cite different types of material.
- Searching techniques when using other bibliographic or location checking services.
- What sort of information is available on other online services.
- The life cycle a request must go through and each of its processing stages.
- An overview of the services offered by the British Library (BL). If the opportunity arises, allow staff to visit the Document Supply Centre in Boston Spa so that they have a better picture of what goes on there.
- If possible arrange a visit to another library that you use regularly for supply to help foster good working relationships.

It is useful for staff to attend training workshops organised by the Forum for Interlending and Information Discovery (FIL) and the regional library services.[1]

Looking outside the department

Because co-operation is a key element in the success of IDS it is vitally important for staff to nurture relationships with other libraries and develop new links. External relations are often the first casualty when staffing levels are reduced in IDS departments, to the detriment of the whole interlending community. It is worth arranging visits to other libraries, being active in local consortia, and encouraging staff to become involved in professional organisations locally and nationally.

Organisation of work in the department

There are various models for arranging how work is organised in the interlending department and some areas that you should consider when assigning tasks.

IT resources

Planning of work in the section needs to fit in with the software that you are using to manage your requests. Make sure that the way you are working follows the fastest workflow possible in your LMS. Plans for your work will also be dependent on the number of PCs you have available at any one time.

Patterns of working

It is advisable to create a pattern of working in the section so that regular tasks are performed in an organised way rather than just doing something when you have time. It is a good idea, for example, to send off new requests as early in the morning as possible as there is a greater possibility that they will be dealt with by your supplier that day or that items will be put into the post for you the same day. The importance of the structure you give to the work of the department will be raised if you have set service standards.

Bibliographic checking

Depending on your staff resources and the number of requests you receive you will need to decide how much intervention is needed on the part of your staff before requests are sent off to suppliers. Some departments take the approach that it is a waste of time to send requests off without verifying the details that the reader has supplied. In other institutions the sheer number of requests means that requests are sent off without confirming the details and that mistakes made by readers will be dealt with when the requests fail and are returned unfulfilled by the supplier. A balanced approach may be advisable.

Entering or checking requests

If you are entering a large number of requests onto your computer system or checking the details entered by readers or other staff it is a good idea to divide this task up among staff where possible. Anyone asked to type in the details of more than about 40 or 50 requests in one go will find that their accuracy decreases, so this job should be shared out.

Choosing suppliers

Choosing the first supplier for a request is the key decision for an efficient service. If you follow a similar pattern when choosing a supplier for all your requests (such as sending everything to the BL) this can easily be applied by all staff. However, if your requests are more complicated and require a better knowledge of the subject area before a decision on the supplier can be made you may wish to assign staff the responsibility of dealing with certain subjects or certain types of material. Some academic libraries, for example, assign requests from specific faculties to the same member of staff so that they build up an expertise in that area. You may also wish to explore IT solutions that can remove any staff involvement in this decision-making, by introducing unmediated requesting based on carefully configured IDS software.

Failed requests and searching for alternative locations

When your normal suppliers have not been able to provide you with the material, you will need to decide how much effort you put into finding alternative locations. Again the work you put into this will depend on your staffing levels and access to databases. Searching for locations could be divided among staff by subject area or left to more senior or experienced staff.

Incoming requests

If your institution is one that receives many requests for loans or copies from your own stock, you can separate out this task and assign it to specific staff in your section. (In a few institutions these tasks are dealt with outside the main IDS section.) Alternatively the work can be shared out among all the staff. If you receive a large number of photocopy requests you may wish to employ casual staff to undertake the copying.

Invoice checking

The IDS section may also be responsible for checking its own invoices for requests before they are passed for payment. In consultation with your financial staff you will need to decide what level of checking to undertake. If you receive a regular invoice from the BL, it will contain an entry for each item supplied, and carrying out a thorough check on each charge is very time-consuming. A more pragmatic approach may be to:

- check that all the request numbers listed are yours;
- check all non-standard or large fees.

This task can easily be shared among staff in the section if there is a lot of checking to do.

Customer care

All the work done in the IDS department should focus on the customer. You are there to provide information readers are having difficulty obtaining and your only constraints should be your budget and time, not a lack of willingness to help.

Communicating with your readers will help keep them on your side and help them to understand the work you have done for them. It may be that people can monitor the progress of their requests on your computer system but if not, be willing to let them know what has happened: do not let interlending turn into a black hole. Email is an ideal way to update people on the progress of requests.

It is worth being honest with readers when you are struggling with requests or where they have asked for something that you have no realistic chance of obtaining. Be prepared to suggest alternatives to your users, such as visits to reference libraries. There is no point battling for months to get a loan copy of an item when there is a perfectly good reference copy in a library nearby. In this way you are emphasising your role as an information provider rather than focusing on the IDS process.

Libraries requesting material from you are your customers too, so do not hold onto their requests for weeks if you do not have the staff to deal with them. It is better to send the requests back with a note to say that you are busy, in case they have other locations to try. Some libraries email the lis-ill email group to alert other libraries that they are short-staffed; UnityWeb and LinkUK allow libraries to indicate when they are 'closed' to incoming requests. Remember that IDS only works if people are fair in their dealing with each other, and think about how you like to be treated by your suppliers.

User education

It is not often that staff from the interlending department are given the opportunity to take part in formal sessions to explain their service to users, but if other staff offer these type of sessions, ensure that your service is mentioned. If you are given the opportunity to take part do not be shy about what you do.

Remember, however, that because of the costs involved in processing IDS requests many organisations will not want to encourage the promotion of the service. You must, therefore, be realistic and do not heavily advertise your service if increases in requests will lead to an impossible strain on your budget or on your staffing.

Informal education of readers will depend largely on how much contact you have with them but, even if you do not operate a front-line desk, with email and telephone it is possible to ensure your advice is passed on.

If you rely on other staff at an information point you should ensure that they are given adequate education on what service you can offer. Make sure that they understand what information you require, and what is dispensable. For instance, they must not accept a request for a journal article without the details of the periodical in which it appeared, but they can accept a book request without the name of the publisher. If staff on the information desk know what you are able to do they will be confident in explaining this to the users and unlikely to create false expectations. To this end some IDS departments offer regular training sessions for all front-line staff.

It is useful to produce guides for your customers which outline the services you are able to offer and what types of information you are able to supply. This means that even if you are not able to meet people directly you can ensure that they are given the correct information. Many libraries offer guides on their Web pages as well as in printed form.

When readers have made a mistake it gives you the perfect opportunity to explain how to quote material successfully to avoid repeating the same type of mistake. This sort of knowledge will be useful to them if they have to prepare a bibliography, as well as when they are submitting their requests to you. If you have used a database to check something, and it is available to them as well, then let them know about it.

Remember that the knowledge you have about other libraries and their collections will make you a useful tool for researchers. If you do build up this sort of skill make sure that other library staff know that you are happy to help when people are trying to locate information.

Service standards

Setting service standards can help you achieve a high level of customer satisfaction. Standards ensure that your service meets a consistent level of quality and speed and your users know what to expect.

The Public Library Service Standards include a target, PLSS5, for the time period from when a request is made to when a reader is informed that it is available. The targets are:

- 50% of requests for books met within 7 days,
- 70% of requests for books met within 15 days,
- 85% of requests for books met within 30 days.[2]

These are reasonable standards which any IDS section should aim to fulfil. You might also like to consider other areas where you can set your own standards.

- *Submitting requests.* Agree to process all requests received from your readers within a set time limit, e.g. all requests received today will be sent off tomorrow.
- *Responding to requests.* Agree to respond to all incoming requests from other libraries within a set time limit.
- *Chasing requests.* Set up mechanisms to ensure that you chase any requests from suppliers that you have not heard anything about within agreed time limits.
- *Communicating with users.* Agree to let your readers know the progress of their requests after a certain period of time.

You may be able to implement some of these standards through your IDS management system.

When you are setting standards, ensure that you are promising to do something that you can actually deliver. You must not foster unrealistic expectations in your users.

Statistics

Keeping statistics is important if you want to monitor the use of your service and its efficiency. You will probably be able to obtain much data from your computer system but you may still need to keep your own spreadsheets for some other information.

You will need to provide statistical information to outside bodies such as a regional library service, or local consortium. Public libraries will also have to submit yearly totals to the Chartered Institute of Public Finance and Accountancy (CIPFA), while academic libraries supply information for the SCONUL survey.

At the most basic level you will need to keep statistics on the number of requests:

- you receive from users;
- you make to suppliers;
- that are successfully filled;
- received from other libraries;
- successfully supplied to other libraries.

You may also consider obtaining statistics on:

- how many requests you send to each supplier;
- how many requests you receive from each requesting library;
- how long both incoming and outgoing requests take to be successfully filled;
- types of requests, e.g. loans, photocopies, theses;
- numbers of special requests, e.g. urgent action, international, copyright-cleared.

Statistics can be a vital tool in the efficient operation of your section. They will help you plan staffing levels and predict busy periods. If you have information on the performance of suppliers they will help you make informed decisions on future requesting patterns. If you have information on the titles and subject areas you are requesting you can feed this into local acquisition policies.

Do not, however, let the keeping of statistics become an onerous task or make collecting them such a burden that it detracts from your main work.

Evaluating the performance of the department

Evaluating how successfully the department is meeting the needs of users is much harder to gauge. Statistics may help in defining some of this.

What proportion of requests that you receive are you fulfilling? What is your failure rate? How many requests do you have to cancel?

Some organisations regularly survey their readers. If yours is one of them you might want to consider including questions on the more subjective question of whether people are satisfied with the service you offer and if they like what you are doing. If the results of a survey show your department in a positive light make sure that they are publicised, and poor results can help you by highlighting the areas that you need to improve.

We have to look outside the British Isles for work on benchmarking of the IDS service, with the aim of establishing best practice and the most efficient ways of working. In Australia in 2001 the National Resource Sharing Working Group carried out a benchmarking study of 97 libraries from all sectors.[3] They looked at:

- turnaround time, and found that the average period from all respondents was 11.5 days;

- fill rate, where they found that the average was 89%; and

- unit cost, where they found that the average was the equivalent of £13.69.

The survey figures make interesting reading and allow other libraries to benchmark their own performance against the average. The purpose of the Australian study was also to identify the key factors in common in all of the most efficient IDS departments. Based on this research they were able to make five recommendations:

- *Examine workflows to ensure that there are as few processing steps as possible.* The most efficient libraries aimed to obtain 90% of their requests from the first library to which they applied.

- *Implement as much automation as possible because the automation of any part of the process was seen to lead to increased efficiency.* This might include getting readers to create their own requests online or supplying material electronically where this was possible.

- *Ensure that staff are well trained in resources and systems.* Staff are the most expensive part of the overall unit costs in any IDS section and therefore need to maximise their skills as 'expert searchers' who are knowledgeable about key resources.

- *Maintain up-to-date holdings information.* Requesting was more efficient when staff were consulting union catalogues with up-to-date records of holdings.

- *Investigate cooperative arrangements with key libraries.*

The study carried out in Australia was based on a similar review carried out some years before among North American libraries by Mary Jackson.[4] While the Australian work was being undertaken another study was set up in the Nordic region.[5]

No detailed study has been undertaken in the British Isles but you could compare the efficiency of the service you offer with other similar libraries by making informal contact with them. Alternatively, you may be able to find appropriate statistical information from the bodies you share your own statistics with, such as CIPFA and SCONUL.[6] Some basic statistical information about IDS can also be obtained from LISU publications.[7]

Financial issues

How much do requests cost?

Financial planning and management require you to have an idea of how much requests cost. But be aware that issues to do with the cost of IDS and how much of that cost should be passed onto readers is often very politically sensitive. On a basic level you can look at how much individual requests cost in your region, your local consortium or through BL. You should add to this the costs your department must meet for subscriptions to any searching services that you have, and transport costs. For the fullest picture, to this must be added the cost of your facilities, the office space and PCs, etc., and, if it is available to you, information on the cost of the staffing involved. If you are ever asked to quantify the cost of a request remember that the answer you give will depend on who is asking the question.

How much to charge

How much of the cost of the request you pass on to your readers will depend on your own funding arrangements and is likely to be a decision that will need to be taken along with senior managers in your institution. It is useful to note that when you are supplying photocopy requests there is a legal requirement that the requester makes a contribution towards the cost.

There is always considerable debate about the appropriate level to charge for IDS services. If you need to review your charges you may wish to compare them with other similar institutions. Informal surveys on charging are often carried out by members of the lis-ill email group.[8]

When setting your charges you can make a distinction between core services and value-added services, such as overseas requests or same-day supply, for which you recoup the full cost. You will also need to decide how you wish to deal with requests that need to be Copyright Cleared, and consider passing on to your user the whole of the copyright royalty fee payable to the publisher.

In some settings you may be able to make a distinction based on what the request is being used for. In an academic library, for example, you may charge a higher rate if material is requested for personal interest rather than for work or study.

Cost versus speed

Choices you make on the suppliers you use or the new services you exploit may well have financial implications. There is often a trade-off between the cost and the speed of the service you are using. Cheaper services will often mean your readers have to wait longer for their requests to be filled and the quality of photocopies may be reduced. Compare, for example, the speed of the commercial services offered by BL with those supplied through a local consortium.

Using a new or alternative service may involve additional staff costs. Requests might, for example, be cheaper from a new service but could involve you checking your requests against another database before sending them, or re-keying information if you are not able to send them directly from your own computer system. This cost in staff time should not be ignored as it may have a significant impact on the speed of your service.

Access versus holdings

The cost of IDS can also be compared with the cost of the alternative: increased spending on local holdings. Is it actually cheaper to cancel a periodical subscription for a less popular title and use document delivery to provide articles for your users on demand? The issue of access versus holdings has been hotly debated in the academic sector, in particular since the Anderson Report of 1994[9] suggested that no library could be expected to meet all the information needs of its users through local holdings. Libraries from all sectors may be able to save money overall through an enhanced use of IDS but will need to ensure that they are not putting unreasonable obstacles in the way of their user's information needs and that any increased reliance on IDS can be met by current staff levels.[10]

Offsetting income against costs

The IDS department is not just a drain on the library budget; it may well also be making some money. Your library charges other libraries for the requests that you supply to them. If you are a member of a consortium such as CONARLS or a regional library service, the charges you make will have been decided by the group. Otherwise any library can set its own rate, but few libraries exceed the BL standard charge. If your library charges more than this you should inform requesting libraries before you supply.

The number of requests a library receives is largely a reflection of the availability of its holdings information in union catalogues. If you are committed to sharing this information, you will increase the number of requests you receive and therefore the income you gain for supplying the material.

Beyond IDS: career development

Many staff remain in IDS for a considerable part of their career because they are interested in the work and committed to it. But, if we are honest, it can be a forgotten area of library work that is under-appreciated by the decision-makers in our institutions. If you are looking for change, you could stay in IDS but move to a different type of library. If you decide you want to move on, make sure you 'sell' the valuable transferable skills that you have obtained. Areas you might consider include:

- general acquisitions work, as many of the processing and bibliographic skills required are very similar to those in IDS;
- front-line services such as circulation work, where your customer-focused approach from IDS will be invaluable;
- systems work, as you will probably have been making heavy use of a variety of IT systems and technology;
- information or reference desk work, where your knowledge of databases and searching for material will be useful.

IDS work also provides an excellent foundation for people who choose to go on to study for qualifications in Librarianship and Information Science.

Notes

1. You may also find it useful to look at the excellent training materials prepared by LIANZA (Library and Information Association of New Zealand Aoetaroa): *Interloans Best Practice Handbook*, 2005: *http://www.lianza.org.nz/about/profile/interloan/interloan_bpwlinks.html*

2. Department for Culture, Media and Sport (2004) *New Public Library Service Standards*, *http://www.culture.gov.uk/global/publications/archive_2004/library_standards.htm*

3. National Resource Sharing Working Group (2001) *Interlibrary Loan and Document Delivery Benchmarking Study*, National Library of Australia, *http://www.nla.gov.au/initiatives/nrswg/illdd_rpt_sum.html*

4. Jackson, Mary E. (1998) *Measuring the Performance of Interlibrary Loan Operations in North American Research and College Libraries.* Washington, DC: Association of Research Libraries.

5. Vattulainen, Pentti (2001) *Nordic Study of Performance Measurement of Interlibrary Loan and Document Delivery Services*, *http://www.nrl.fi/nvbf/nordicpm.htm*

6. You will normally either need to register or be a contributor to see this type of information. For CIPFA see *http://www.cipfastats.net/*; for SCONUL see *http://www.sconul.ac.uk/pubs_stats/stats.html*

7. See in particular: *LISU Annual Library Statistics 2004*, *http://info.lut.ac.uk/departments/dils/lisu/pages/publications/als04.html*

8. For a more complete study of charging among academic libraries made in 1999 see: Clinton, P. (1999) 'Charging users for interlibrary loans in UK university libraries: a new survey', *Interlending and Document Supply* 27(1): 17–29.

9. Joint Funding Councils' Libraries Review (1994) *Report of the Group on a National/Regional Strategy for Library Provision for Researchers (The Anderson Report)*, HEFCE. *http://www.ukoln.ac.uk/services/elib/papers/other/anderson/*

10. For a more complete discussion on this issue see, for instance: Line, Maurice B. (1995) 'Opinion paper: access as a substitute for holdings: false ideal or costly reality?', *Interlending and Document Supply* 23(2): 28–30; Blagden, John (1998) 'Opinion paper: access versus holdings', *Interlending and Document Supply* 26(3): 140–3; Boyle, Frances and Davies, Mary (1999) 'Access versus holdings: document delivery realities', *Electronic Library* 17(2): 105–13.

11

Copyright

Jean Bradford

I would like to thank Charles Oppenheim for his help in reading this chapter and for his comments and advice. I am responsible for the final text.

Introduction

IDS librarians need to know enough about copyright so that they understand what the law allows them to do on behalf of their users, and for the users of other libraries. They do not need to know about the application of copyright legislation in other settings, but, because IDS staff have to know something, very often they undertake responsibility for wider issues involving copyright within their institution. This chapter will only consider those aspects of copyright which have an impact on IDS operations. There are other books which give good advice about copyright for librarians and these should be consulted for a wider treatment of the subject. A list is attached to this chapter as suggestions for further reading. The question of copying unpublished material is more likely to be the concern of archivists and special collections librarians. However, IDS librarians in universities may be asked about copying theses sent on inter-library loan, so this topic is included in this chapter. Also included is a consideration of the copyright issues affecting the supply of articles from electronic publications.

It should always be remembered that copyright is a legal matter and this chapter does not attempt to provide legal advice about copyright.

Legislation

There are two Acts of Parliament which are the foundation of the law governing copyright. These are:

- The Copyright, Designs and Patents Act 1988 (CDPA 1988)
- The Copyright (Visually Impaired Persons) Act 2002

The CDPA 1988 has been amended by a number of Statutory Instruments (SIs) since 1988, most recently in October 2003, when a major change was introduced. The SI 2003/2498 Copyright and Related Rights Regulations 2003 was the means of implementing a European Directive on Copyright into UK law and anything written about copyright before 31 October 2003 should be treated with caution. Cornish[1] and Norman[2] list all the relevant SIs, and texts of all the legislation can be found on the Office of Public Sector Information website.[3]

What is copyright?

Copyright is the protection given by the law to those who create original works. Works do not just mean printed books and journals; artistic works, dramatic performances, radio and television broadcasts, and Internet pages are all among the works protected by copyright. There is a balance to be kept between the rights of those who create works and those who want to access them. The most important thing to note, however, is that the only person who has a right to make a copy of the work is its creator, or anyone to whom the creator has assigned or licensed the right, for example a publisher. Anyone else who makes a copy only has 'defences' allowed under legislation which they can use if their copying is challenged. Unless permission has been given, then copies can only be made relying on the defences provided in the legislation.

Exceptions provided to individuals by legislation

1. *Fair dealing for research or private study.* This is the most familiar exception. Fair dealing is not defined but it is generally accepted as meaning that the interests of the owner of a work are not harmed by the copying. It allows copying of all or a substantial part of a work for research for a non-commercial purpose or private study. Since the

change in the law in October 2003, copying for private study must also be for a non-commercial purpose. The person making the copy does not have to be registered formally on a course of study to qualify for the exception for non-commercial research or private study. There is some general advice on the Web pages of the Patent Office[4] and some useful Frequently Asked Questions on the British Library's Web pages.[5] Users should be referred to sources such as these as it is their responsibility to decide whether their purpose is commercial or not and whether what they want to copy is likely to be considered fair dealing or not.

2. *Fair dealing for criticism or review.* If someone is writing a review or a criticism of a work, he or she is permitted to include extracts of it; otherwise the review may not be comprehensible. There are two conditions. Full details of the item being reviewed must be included and the work must be legally available to the public.

3. *Fair dealing for reporting current events.* This exception allows for copies to be made in order to report current events. Photographs are not covered by this exception and so should not be included. The source of the copies must also be acknowledged.

There are also some exceptions provided to educational establishments, for example allowing the inclusion of copies in examination questions or answers. For more information about these, it is best to refer to the books listed at the end of the chapter.

What copying can librarians do for their patrons?

The relevant sections of the CDPA 1988 are 37–43, headed *Libraries and Archives.* Any copies made under these provisions are often referred to as 'Library privilege copies', as the law allows librarians to make copies for users and other libraries provided that they adhere to the conditions laid down in these Sections.

Prescribed and non-prescribed libraries

The CDPA 1988 introduced a distinction between prescribed and non-prescribed libraries. (The distinction is defined in SI 1989 no. 1212.) Prescribed libraries are:

- public libraries;
- national libraries including the Bodleian Library, Oxford, and the University of Cambridge Library;
- libraries in educational establishments;
- parliamentary and government libraries;
- local authority libraries, such as a Members Library for local councillors
- NHS Libraries;
- any library whose purpose is to facilitate the study of a wide range of subjects;
- any library outside the UK which facilitates the study of the same range of subjects.

Libraries which are part of an organisation which is profit making cannot be prescribed libraries.

Although all libraries may supply copies to their users, only prescribed libraries may request and supply copies which are to be added to the stock of the requesting library. Conditions are also attached to the supply of copies, whether they are obtained for the end-user or to be added to stock.

Amount that librarians can copy

The CDPA does define the amount which librarians may copy. Section 38 says that a librarian may make 'one copy of an article in a periodical' without infringing copyright, but this is the only limit which is given. For other types of material no limits are defined, the Act just says that a librarian may supply a copy of part of them. No multiple copying is allowed, so only one copy can be supplied. If a user wishes to have copies of more than one article in an issue, then the librarian must request a loan of the whole issue or permission must be sought for the copying. In some libraries, for example in NHS libraries, a licence allows copying of more than one article from an issue. It is important for IDS librarians to know if a licence is in place in their organisation. A section on Licences is included later in this chapter.

Conditions for supplying copies to users
Declaration forms

The user requesting a librarian to supply a copy must sign a declaration form and the text of the declaration is included in the legislation. The most recent can be found in the Copyright and Related Rights Regulations 2003 (SI 2003 No. 2498). On the declaration the user states among other things that the purpose of the copy is for non-commercial research or study and that he or she has not received a copy from any librarian previously. The most important statement is that if the copy is found to be an infringing copy, then the user is responsible for this and not the librarian supplying it. Librarians should be satisfied that the reader making the declaration has not done so falsely; however, there is no obligation for them to investigate the circumstances of every request. If the librarian knows that the declaration is false, the copy should not be supplied. The librarian must receive the copyright declaration *before* the copy is given to the reader. As users now have to sign to declare that the copy is required for non-commercial purposes in order to have a library privilege copy, IDS librarians must receive the declaration before the request is sent to the supplying library, so that they can be sure that the request is appropriate for this form of supply. The Circle of Officers of National and Regional Library Systems (Conarls) has drawn up the following form of words which should be used when requesting a copy from another library:

> Please supply a photocopy. It is for non-commercial research or private study and a signed declaration to that effect is held by this Library.

BLDSC has asked all its customers to sign a new agreement, which includes the responsibility of the requesting library for obtaining a signed declaration before sending the request. Procedures for obtaining copyright declarations place a bureaucratic burden on IDS librarians, but it is important that the services which they offer are seen to comply with the law. Signed declarations can be sent to IDS sections by fax, which can help to speed up the process. Once signed declarations have been received, they must be stored by the library. No time limit is given in the legislation for storage.

Costs

The CDPA 1988 says that the reader must pay for the copy being supplied to them. The charge must cover the costs of making the copy and may include a contribution to the running costs of the supplying library. The Act does not say anything about how the charges are to be made, whether the reader must pay directly or whether any costs may be charged back to the reader's department in a college or university or commercial organisation. The important point for IDS librarians to remember is that there is no such thing as a free copy, and the supplying library must charge the requesting library for any copies supplied.

Copies for judicial proceedings

There are no limits placed on the amount that can be copied of items needed to support cases in law courts or parliamentary proceedings. The provision for this is made in Section 45 of CDPA 1988, where it states:

> S.45 (1) Copyright is not infringed by anything done for the purposes of parliamentary or judicial proceedings.

This is comprehensive and allows for copies to be made for use in a number of different settings. If a copy is required for judicial proceedings and a librarian is asked to supply it, the copyright declaration described above is not required or appropriate. The CDPA 1988 does not state that any declaration must be signed, but it would be sensible for IDS librarians to ask for a statement to the effect that the copy is required for judicial proceedings when the reader makes the request, so that there is a record which explains why no other declaration has been kept. This statement should also form part of the request when it is sent to the supplying library.

Copying for library stock

Section 41 of CDPA 1988 allows only prescribed libraries to add copies to their stock under certain conditions. If several articles from the same issue of a journal are required or a substantial part of another type of material, librarians must have made an attempt to contact the rights-holder to ask for permission. If they have been unable to identify the rights-holder, they are able to obtain the copy under this provision. If only one article is required or only a small part of a book is needed, there is no requirement to seek permission. Prescribed libraries may ask other prescribed libraries for copies which they wish to add to stock and the supplying library must charge for them.

Copies for preservation and replacement

Section 42 of CDPA 1988 is the relevant section when copies are required for repair and conservation. A library or archive may wish to make a copy of an original item in their stock, for example in cases where the original is fragile and in poor condition, or where it has been lost, or when pages have been torn out. This is only possible when it is not reasonably practical to buy another copy and the copy being replaced or repaired is in the reference collection. This means that copies made under these provisions may not be lent to users of the library. If the copy was originally kept in the lending collection, it should be transferred to the reference collection once it has been repaired. It is possible to ask for permission from the rights-holder, should the library wish to continue lending it. If a library wishes to obtain copies for these purposes, it must state that their original copy is lost or damaged, that it is not practicable to buy another copy and that the work will be for reference only. The supplying library must make a charge for supplying the copy and this charge should cover the cost of supplying the copy plus a contribution to the general expenses of the library.

Making copies for visually impaired people (VIPs)

The Copying (Visually Impaired Persons) Act 2003 is the law which allows VIPs, who are prevented from using material because of its format, to make copies. Copies made under this Act are called 'Accessible Copies'. They can be in a format such as Braille or in an electronic format, or audio copies on tape or CD, whichever format is most suitable for the person using it. The only conditions are:

1. The person must either own or have lawful use of the item copied. This means that librarians may make copies of material in their stock for VIP users and VIPs may use the copy only so long as they are members of that library. For example, students on a course may have an accessible copy while they are following the course. Once they finish the course and no longer have access to the copy in the library, the accessible copy must be destroyed.
2. The work must not be available commercially in the required format.
3. If the work is a piece of music, the copy must not involve recording a performance of the work.
4. The copy must be clearly identified with the bibliographic details of the item copied.
5. There must be a clear statement on the copy that it has been made in accordance with the 2003 Act.

Educational establishments and not-for-profit organizations can make multiple accessible copies and supply them to VIPs. These organizations are also allowed to lend accessible copies to each other. They must keep records of all the copies made and to whom these copies have been supplied. They must also record the copies which have been lent to other institutions and allow the copyright owners or their representatives to access these records. They must also notify the copyright owners of any copies transferred or lent to another organisation. It is in the lending and transferring of accessible copies where IDS librarians may be involved. The REVEAL database includes locations for copies in alternative formats and this is included in the UNITY database. As more copies become available, IDS librarians in schools, colleges and universities as well as in public libraries may find themselves receiving increasing numbers of requests from users who wish to borrow accessible copies.

Unpublished material

Making copies of unpublished material is much more likely to be done by archivists and librarians in special collections, and the best guide for this topic is Padfield's book.[6] However, one type of material about which IDS librarians are likely to be asked is theses. It is important to remember that copying theses is the same as copying any type of unpublished material. It is not possible to make a copy of any thesis if it was published before it was deposited in the library – unlikely, but some degrees are awarded on the basis of published work. Copies cannot be made if the author has expressly forbidden copying. Copies can only be made for individuals for non-commercial private study and research for non-commercial purposes, and a declaration must be signed. However, in most universities in the UK, as part of the process of awarding a higher degree, the author signs a suitable permission form allowing a thesis to be copied and lent at the discretion of the university librarian. It may also include permission for the BLDSC to make a microform copy and supply copies from the microform copy in its possession. This means that original theses may be copied and lent and that BLDSC can make them available through the British Thesis Service.

Electronic signatures

The requirement to receive a signed copyright declaration before sending a request to a supplier is a great hindrance for IDS librarians, especially when their library management system allows readers to place requests electronically, or when they wish to use Web pages to allow readers to initiate requests. Using electronic signatures would streamline the whole process and speed the supply of the article to end-users, many of whom are baffled by the need to sign a declaration. Electronic signatures are now legal in contracts under the Electronic Communications Act, 2000. The Libraries and Archives Copyright Alliance (LACA) sought clarification from the Patent Office about using the provisions of the 2000 Act to allow electronic signatures on copyright declarations.[7] The outcome of this was positive. Some people have suggested that the username and password which requesters use to identify themselves to the library management system is sufficient to count as an electronic signature. The Electronic Communications Act, 2000, however, sets a more rigorous standard. Section 7 states that for an electronic signature to be counted as valid, the author must be able to demonstrate that it is authentic, i.e. the person who claims to have sent it did indeed do so, and that it has integrity, i.e. that it cannot have been amended on route. It is very unlikely that usernames and passwords will meet this test. Library systems suppliers need to develop their products to meet these standards, so that electronic signatures can be used.

Licences

So far this chapter has been concerned with what the law allows. The law also permits licensing schemes to extend its provisions. For example, both higher education/further education (HE/FE) institutions and the NHS have licences from the Copyright Licensing Agency (CLA) which extend what is allowed by the legislation, e.g. by allowing the making of multiple copies for use in class. There are a number of other licences which cover the copying of specific types of material, e.g. maps. It is important to check which are available in your institution.

Libraries that wish to supply copies to other libraries in response to requests for copies for the purpose of commercial research can do this by taking out a Licence with the CLA. Two are available:

1. *Transactional Document Delivery Licence.* This allows a publisher to set a price for the copyright royalty to be paid for copying articles for each of their titles. This means that each request must be checked against a spreadsheet provided by the CLA to find out what charge should be made for copying that article. The royalty is charged in

addition to the charge for making the copy. The disadvantage of this licence is that each request must be checked, and this takes staff time. This is the licence used by BLDSC for its copyright cleared service, but only a few libraries besides BLDSC have taken it out. It is difficult to know which libraries provide a service for commercial copies besides BLDSC.

2. *Low Volume Document Delivery Licence.* This has been devised for libraries which wish to supply fewer than 100 copies per month for commercial research. The library decides how many copies per month it will supply and pays the CLA in advance a flat fee for each copy. The disadvantage of this licence is that if the library does not sell as many copies as it has paid for, it will lose money.

There is another licence, the CLA Library Sticker Scheme, which has been devised to allow libraries to sell a sticker to a user who wishes to make a copy for commercial research using library self-service photocopiers. This is designed solely for the needs of 'walk-in' users and cannot be used for document supply. This is a pity, as there is a need for something similar, to allow libraries to make the occasional copy for commercial research in response to a request from another library.

Copyright in the electronic environment

The answers to many of the questions about copyright in the electronic world are the same as those to questions about copying of printed material. The content is protected by copyright and the fact that it is made available in an electronic format does not alter the answer. However, in the electronic environment it is more likely that libraries have obtained their electronic materials under licence from the publisher. In these circumstances it is the licence, which they have signed, which will govern the access to the electronic product. This is because licences are regulated by the law of contract which takes precedence over copyright legislation. Licences usually specify how many concurrent users may access the product and who is authorized to use it. If the licence states that supplying copies of articles to other libraries is prohibited, then no copy can be supplied. This means that IDS librarians, who receive requests from other libraries for copies of articles that are only held electronically, must check to see what the licence for the product being requested states. There are model licences, e.g. that produced by NESLi2. NESLi2 is the umbrella organisation which negotiates with publishers on behalf of the Joint Information Systems Committee (JISC) for

HE/FE institutions and so a number of journals subscribed to by libraries in the HE/FE community will be covered by this. In the NESLi2 Licence, Section 3.1.3.6 states that the Licensee may:

> supply to an authorised user of another library (whether by post, fax or secure electronic transmission, using Ariel or its equivalent, whereby the electronic file is deleted immediately after printing) a single paper copy of an electronic original of an individual document.[8]

IDS librarians must check thoroughly before supplying a copy and liaise with their colleagues responsible for the provision of electronic materials, if necessary.

Computer programs and technological protection methods

As well as protecting the content of an electronic document, copyright legislation also protects the computer program supporting it, as computer programs are included in the works covered by the legislation. Electronic publications may also be classified as databases in which case they will also be protected by the Database Right, which is given to databases that 'have been assembled as a result of substantial investment in obtaining, verifying or presenting the contents'.[9] Various technological protection methods have been devised to protect electronic publications from alteration and unauthorised use, e.g. encryption. Since October 2003, it has been an offence to tamper with any protection system. Digital rights management systems provide information identifying the work, for example statements about the author and title. Any attempt to remove these systems has also been an offence since October 2003. There is a very cumbersome and bureaucratic procedure for those who believe that a system is preventing them from accessing something to which they believe they are entitled.

Summary

This is only a brief outline which has focused on issues which IDS librarians may encounter. The following are sources of information which they may find helpful.

Further reading

Books

Cornish, Graham (2004) *Copyright: Interpreting the Law for Libraries, Archives and Information Services*, 4th edn. London: Facet Publishing (1856045080).

Norman, Sandy (2004) *Practical Copyright for Information Professionals: the CILIP Handbook*. London: Facet Publishing (1856044904).

Padfield, Timothy (2004) *Copyright for Archivists and Users of Archives*, 2nd edn. London: Facet Publishing (1903365139).

Websites

The British Library. The British Library has a list of frequently asked questions and other useful information on its website at
http://www.bl.uk/services/information/copyrightfaq.html [accessed 16 April 2005]

The Copyright Licensing Agency
http://www.cla.co.uk/index.html [accessed 16 April 2005]

Libraries and Archives Copyright Alliance (LACA)
http://www.cilip.org.uk/committees/laca/laca.html [accessed 16 April 2005]

The Patent Office. This is the government department responsible for copyright legislation.
http://www.patent.gov.uk/ [accessed 16 April 2005]

Mailing list

Lis-copyseek is a closed mailing list hosted by JISCmail for staff who have copyright responsibilities in their institutions. It is an invaluable source of help. More information about this list can be found at
http://www.jiscmail.ac.uk/lists/lis-copyseek.html [accessed 16 April 2005]

Notes

1. Cornish, Graham (2004) *Copyright: Interpreting the Law for Libraries, Archives and Information Services*, 4th edn. London: Facet Publishing (1856045080).
2. Norman, Sandy (2004) *Practical Copyright for Information Professionals: the CILIP Handbook*. London: Facet Publishing (1856044904).

3. *http://www.opsi.gov.uk/legislation/about_legislation.htm*
4. *http://www.intellectual-property.gov.uk/std/resources/copyright/index.htm*
5. *http://www.bl.uk/services/information/copyrightfaq.html*
6. Padfield, Timothy (2004) *Copyright for Archivists and Users of Archives*, 2nd edn. London: Facet Publishing (1856045129).
7. *http://www.cilip.org.uk/committees/laca/laca.html* [accessed 16 April 2005].
8. *http://www.nesli2.ac.uk/model.htm*
9. Cornish, *op. cit.*, p. 140.

12

International borrowing and lending

Jill Evans

Requesting material

British libraries usually approach libraries abroad only when a search of all UK libraries has been completed. This means that the British Library (BL) has sent a No UK Location report (NUKL), and the requesting library has completed any further checks which it thinks are appropriate. Extending a search abroad varies in terms of cost, success rate and supply time.

Consult with your reader

Because of the costs – in money and staff time – of applying abroad, you should:

- Ensure that the reader still requires the item.
- Make sure the reader is prepared to wait. He or she may have a limited schedule in which the work is of use to their research or study.
- Inform the reader that overseas loans are invariably supplied for reference use only within the requesting library's premises, and cannot be transferred to another library.
- Warn the reader that the item may only be available for a short time, and that it may not be possible to renew a loan; you may decide to postpone the loan to a more convenient date.
- Clarify who is to pay for the item. Some libraries absorb the cost of international loans within the IDS budget, whereas others require the reader to pay the charges themselves.

Bibliographical accuracy

Ensure that the bibliographical details are correct and adequate. In particular, if the item is not in the English language, confirm that the reader can use it if it is in a foreign language.

Next step?

You must now decide whether to ask your regional library service to help with the request, apply to the BL's Worldwide Search service (WWS), use the services of a consortium such as OCLC or RLG Shares, or deal with the request yourself. Individual libraries will have their own policies. WWS is perceived to be costly, but 'do-it-yourself' international requesting can be very expensive in staff time, both in the IDS department and in the Finance Office.

Regional library headquarters

Many public libraries prefer to 'funnel' their requests through a regional library headquarters, which will process requests on behalf of local libraries. An example is the Inter Library Services of the National Library of Scotland. It receives location requests from Scottish public, academic, school and special libraries plus other UK and overseas institutions. The majority of requests for international searching emanate from the Scottish public library sector. The requests are received electronically by email, fax or Ariel and occasionally by post. Location checks are performed using a variety of electronic resources such as COPAC, OCLC Worldcat, and the US Research Libraries Group collaborative and cross-sectoral electronic catalogue called Eureka. The supplied items are generally sent directly to the requesting library.

British Library Document Supply Worldwide Searches

The request may be submitted to British Library Document Supply Worldwide Searches (BLDS-WWS) in Boston Spa by specifying WWS as the search level in your application form. Generally, BLDS-WWS checks OCLC Worldcat, appropriate national libraries and union catalogues, and other collaborative resources depending on the type of material, e.g. international standards and theses. Once the item has been located, BLDS-WWS allocate the request a unique WWS number. They order it electronically through OCLC Worldcat, or use a multi-part paper form for posting to the overseas library. BLDS-WWS inform the requesting library of this number, to enable the progress of the request to be tracked. The paper request is sent by BLDS-WWS to the country of publication, generally to the national library. BLDS-WWS send progress reports via the Replies Intray throughout the lifetime of the request.

If a library can supply the item, they send it to BLDS-WWS, who forward it to the requesting library. The consultation period is 3 weeks. It is sometimes possible to request a renewal of the consultation period, for a small charge. At the end of the consultation period the requesting library returns the loan to BLDS-WWS, by registered post. It is then returned to the supplying library. Photocopies for retention are also supplied by BLDS-WWS.

At the time of writing, an international loan using BLDS-WWS costs £47.80. A photocopy costs £44.25 plus VAT. A charge of £15.50 plus VAT is made for an unsuccessful application abroad. All charges are clearly listed on the BLDS monthly statement to the requesting library, and payment is made on the invoice for other BL services.

RLG Shares

Some university libraries in the UK belong to the Consortium of Research Libraries (CURL). Certain CURL libraries have joined the US initiative Shares, made available by the Research Libraries Group (RLG). This is a cross-sectoral activity enabling Shares partners to supply material on loan, or retention copies of articles, at a financially more attractive rate. At the time of writing, the loan costs between continents is £15.90 and the supply of articles for retention is £5.64. RLG Shares partners are located in the US, Canada, UK, Australia, Europe and New Zealand, and their holdings are listed in the EUREKA database.

OCLC PICA

Some British libraries are members of OCLC and use the OCLC ILL Service Web interface. It is based on Worldcat, which allows the user to find potential lenders and apply direct over the Web. You can identify preferred providers, who are automatically prioritised in future location searches. OCLC members around the world usually deal with fellow members' requests very promptly. Payment can be made in International Federation of Library Associations (IFLA) vouchers or through OCLC's ILL Fee Management service (IFM).

Location searching

Union catalogues from the country of publication are a good starting point for an independent application. (The Appendix to this chapter lists a number of gateways to foreign union catalogues.) Tracing a library online catalogue is best achieved through a resource such as Libweb Index. A clue to the holding library may appear in the publication details, for instance it might be a University of Hong Kong Working Paper.

It is usually easy to log onto the website of the organisation and search its OPAC. Many libraries allow you to switch to English for at least part of their website – often you just look for a small Union flag. A search of the library website should also give you the contact details for the IDS department, and possibly a statement on policy and prices for loans to other libraries. Otherwise you may need to use a general email address for the library. It is helpful to the supplying library to 'cut and paste' the OPAC record into the email message. State the options of payment methods available to you (more on this later in the chapter), and enquire if the library would consider supplying the item on an international loan. It is also helpful to confirm that the return airmail postage will be met, and offer a guarantee that the item will be for library use only. Many libraries will send articles by fax, Ariel or in PDF format, as well as by post.

If the library does not have a presence on the website, it is acceptable to search for the department from which the publication originated, e.g. the Faculty of Music, or the author(s) of the work. Most authors are delighted to receive interest in their work or research, so an enquiry is often successful.

Using ILL lists

The use of LIS-ILL distribution lists is another option to request material from abroad. A popular US list is *http:// ILL-L@listserv.it.northwestern. edu*; the joining instructions are fairly self-explanatory. Libraries send the bibliographical information, plus request number, in an email message and post it to the list. State the proposed payment method in the message, especially if the preferred method is IFLA vouchers. Many libraries respond immediately so it is advisable to secure the details of one library that is able to supply the item, and then inform the other libraries in a joint email that the request has been satisfied.

Donation of items by the supplying library

Occasionally an item may be given as a donation. Requesting libraries have different policies on the final destination of the item. Some consider that a significant amount of library staff time has been absorbed locating and retrieving the item, so the item is added to the library's stock for use by other readers. Other libraries consider that more library staff time will be used with cataloguing, processing and shelving the item, so they may prefer the requestor to retain the item. It is professional and courteous to inform the supplying library of the final destination of their publications – doing so ensures that a spirit of co-operation continues worldwide.

Supplying items to overseas libraries

To lend or not to lend?

Libraries have the option to decide if they wish to supply items abroad or not. It is advisable to provide information on loans policy and procedures on your library's website. You should state clearly material not available for loan, e.g. 'all pre-1900 publications', 'local studies collections', and spell out whether you will lend or copy your theses and dissertations. State if IFLA vouchers are acceptable, and your scale of charges.

Direct supply

If you wish to supply an item directly to the requesting library, contact them to say how long you can lend the item for, and confirm that they are willing to accept it on condition it is used in the library only. If the requesting library has supplied an email address it is advisable to send an email informing them of the despatch date of the item. This ensures that the requesting library is aware of the imminent arrival of the loan.

Supplying/using RLG Shares

Requests emanating from the RLG Shares program are subject to an unobtrusive service-level agreement with turnaround times for supplying or denying responses. Participants use the ILL Manager system, which enables requests to be submitted, searched, located and requested, and the holding library replies, supplies or denies the request within a specified time-frame.

Supplying at the request of the BL

If the BL cannot supply an item from its own stock, it may forward the green request form to other UK libraries, often on a rota. The supplying library sends the item direct to the requesting library. The BL refunds postage costs but does not make a payment for the loan as such.

Payment for international loans and photocopies

BLDS-WWS

All international work co-ordinated through the BL appears on a library's monthly usage statement, and is invoiced or credited with the rest of the BL work for that month's activity.

IFLA vouchers

Some libraries opt to purchase IFLA vouchers, which are a common currency worldwide, to pay the costs of library transactions. Libraries purchase vouchers from the IFLA office at a cost of 8 Euros for a full voucher representing one loan transaction or up to 15 pages of photocopying. A half voucher (4 Euros) is added to pay for a photocopy that exceeds 15 pages. Each voucher, made of plastic, has a six-digit number, and may be re-used repeatedly. The procedure is that Library A in Wales borrows an item from Library B in Africa, and sends a voucher in advance of receipt of the loan or with the item's return. Library B in Africa wishes to request an item from Library C in the US so uses the same voucher to pay the cost of the transaction. Thus, the IFLA voucher may supply items throughout many continents in the world. Libraries may redeem surplus vouchers by contacting the IFLA office, who will reimburse the 4 and 8 Euros costs plus charge a small handling cost of 12 Euros. (All prices are those that applied at the time of writing.) Some form of electronic IFLA voucher is under discussion.

OCLC PICA

OCLC's ILL service includes Interlibrary Loan Fee Management (IFM). All the charges for material supplied and received during the year are calculated and included in an annual statement, which can be paid on one invoice.

RLG Shares payments

The costs of items supplied or received using Shares are calculated in a financial management package on ILL Manager. Libraries are issued annually with either a cheque for supplying more items than they have borrowed, or an invoice if they have borrowed more than they have supplied.

Invoices and foreign currency payments

It is expensive for the supplying library to raise an invoice and process cheque payments. The requesting library will also incur bank charges in processing cheques in foreign currencies, often for rather small amounts. This can lead to friction between IDS and the library's financial administration. IFLA vouchers and credit card payments are usually easier and cheaper.

Credit card payments

Credit cards are a convenient means of paying for interlibrary transactions not covered by IFLA vouchers. Library policies on the use of credit card vary, but credit card details should *never* be sent by email. A fax to the Finance Office or IDS Department should be secure, and some institutions have secure websites through which payment may be made. An alternative approach is to set up an account arrangement under which a customer agrees to provide a credit card number to the supplying library and debits can be made up to an agreed maximum amount. Your library would require suitable security checks to be in place before using this payment option.

Conclusion

International IDS is a small part of most libraries' work – indeed, some institutions neither borrow from abroad nor lend abroad. However, it plays an important part in the free flow of information around the world and is a very practical demonstration of international co-operation.

Appendix: useful websites

The Higher Education and Research Opportunities in the United Kingdom (HERO) website provides a comprehensive list of worldwide resources and OPACs:
http://www.hero.ac.uk/uk/reference_and_subject_resources/resources/ worldwide_library_resources3796.cfm
Libweb Index lists national university college and major public libraries worldwide: *http://lists.webjunction.org/libweb/*
Libraries in higher and further education, and OCLC members, have access to Worldcat, which covers hundreds of libraries in the US and Canada, and also some collections in Latin America, Europe, Asia and Australasia: *http://www.oclc.org/worldcat/default.htm*
Karlsruhe Virtual Catalogue links to German universities, and a number of national libraries worldwide: *http://www.ubka.uni-karlsruhe.de/ hylib/en/kvk.html*
National Library Catalogues Worldwide links alphabetically by country: *http://www.library.uq.edu.au/natlibs/*
GABRIEL, European National Libraries' OPACs: *http://libraries .theeuropeanlibrary.org/libraries_en.xml*
ComElcat, Hungarian academic library catalogues: *http://www.kozelkat .iif.hu/index.english.html*
Italian OPAC Direct connects Italian universities and research site: *http://www.aib.it/aib/opac/repertorio.htm*
Library of Congress, an interface to millions of records: *http://catalog .loc.gov/*

13

A look at the future

Jean Bradford and Jenny Brine

It is not easy to make accurate predictions about future developments – there are numerous examples where hindsight tells us how wrong we can be. So we are writing this chapter with some trepidation. Some developments may grow from things we already know about, but others will come unexpectedly. A look at the future may highlight the first type of development but we can only warn readers to keep their eyes open for surprises.

Technology

Interlending and document supply (IDS) is heavily dependent on the available technologies, whether an efficient postal service or near-universal email. Technology has been a driver of change and development in the past and we can be confident that it will continue to be so. So what might we expect from it?

e-Books

The impact of e-journals has been discussed in earlier chapters. There is a growing number of e-books, although the days of large numbers of individuals taking an e-book reader to the beach loaded with the latest Harry Potter novel have yet to emerge. There are several suppliers, for example NetLibrary, and there are different models to allow access to their list of e-books. So far their market has been mainly that for student textbooks and reference works. In the print environment, many libraries would not make this sort of material available for interlibrary loan, either because of high student demand or because it was available for library use only. However, it has always been possible to copy a chapter of a printed book or an entry from an encyclopaedia in response to a request from another library – will this still be the case with e-books? At present the use of e-books by users who are not members of the subscribing library is usually not permitted by the contract. The answer to questions about copying will be the same as for e-journals: it will depend on the contract that has been signed. As more of our collections become electronic only, how do we provide access to them? Will the Legal Deposit Libraries Act 2003, which is the law concerning the deposit of electronic publications, help? IDS librarians will need to monitor this carefully and make their views known. This will mean making sure that colleagues in acquisitions sections are made aware of the need to provide access for IDS in the electronic world, just as it has been possible in the print environment, as well as lobbying externally. In addition, a large number of books that are out of copyright are available freely via the Internet, and this is likely to increase.

e-Theses

Print copies of theses are usually kept in the Special Collections of academic libraries, and the British Thesis service at the British Library Document Supply Centre (BL) makes some PhD theses available on microfilm. Both formats pose problems, so accessing theses electronically would be a benefit to users and to IDS librarians alike. The Joint Information Systems Committee (JISC) has funded three projects to explore the problems and issues of the deposit and management of e-theses. There are concerns about security, as it is essential to protect e-theses from plagiarism. However, e-theses are certain to happen in the UK. Access to them may be provided through an institution's open access repository (see below). This development will allow researchers to go straight to a thesis they wish to read, and thus reduce the number requested on IDS.

Institutional repositories

These electronic repositories will include a wide range of material in addition to the e-theses discussed above. At present a number of universities in the USA have set up repositories. In the UK the SHERPA Project[1] is encouraging development in British universities. The aim is to persuade researchers in an institution to deposit copies of their work in their institution's repository, so that they are freely available to anyone over the Internet. In addition to e-theses, a repository may include working papers, papers delivered at conferences and copies of journal articles. One possibility is that draft versions may be deposited so that an author may receive feedback on work in progress. Copyright is a concern: will it be possible for articles accepted for publication in journals for which a subscription is charged also to be deposited and freely available? A number of publishers have already agreed to permit this.[2] Institutional repositories are another development which may have an impact on the number of requests made to IDS librarians, as users will be able to access items directly without needing an intermediary.

Open access publishing

Institutional repositories are one aspect of the search for alternative models of publishing the results of research. As the cost of journal subscriptions has increased, there has been increased pressure on library budgets, which have not increased at the same rate as journal prices. Another model is for authors to pay the cost of publication in a journal, which is then available over the Internet free of charge. Such journal titles are listed in the Directory of Open Access Journals, and their number is growing.[3] This is one method of providing access freely to the results of research which is often funded from public funds, but again it will have an impact on the number of IDS requests, as users will be able to access these articles for themselves. We can expect that new relationships will develop between publishers, authors and libraries. IDS librarians will find that they will be working with others in new ways.

Unmediated requests

The developments discussed above may seem to be of most interest to IDS librarians in special or academic libraries where researchers are the heaviest users of IDS services. But the need to support lifelong learning means that those in public libraries will also have to keep up to date with these developments. Unmediated requesting is another development that will also impact on all IDS librarians. The BL has just introduced a service, British Library Direct, which allows members of the public to request copies directly, and to pay by credit card.[4]

It is already possible to purchase individual articles from publishers on a pay-per-view basis. Should we do this on behalf of our readers using institutional credit cards? If readers are being charged for their requests, it does not matter where we obtain the copy, so long as it arrives in time for our customer to use. Users will see no difference between a copy bought directly from the publisher and a copy delivered as a traditional photocopy from another library. However, the way in which the article is delivered from the publisher may prevent us passing it on to a third party. Therefore, the library may need to find ways to fund the purchase of articles when our users have to pay themselves.

Chapter 4 described projects such as Wisdom, which allow users of public libraries to request items directly from participating libraries. It is likely that there will be more such schemes and that they will include libraries from all sectors. Union catalogues will be the basis for these unmediated schemes, as well as being essential tools for peer-to-peer lending. IDS staff will still be needed to make sure that the user receives the correct item – even if the request can be placed directly, the item required still needs to be retrieved and prepared for despatch.

Access to little used material

All libraries have to make decisions about what to include in their collections. As new material is added, older material may have to be withdrawn to make room. Older material, kept in stores, is being discarded as the amount of space allocated to the library is reduced and used in different ways, for example to allow the installation of computers. Everyone welcomes the new services which all libraries, including public libraries, are now able to provide, but the risk is that material is being discarded without any policy being in place to make sure that there is a copy still available somewhere. Copyright libraries have a responsibility to preserve the printed record, but is it right to leave it just to these few institutions? We believe that we need a national strategy for this sort of collection management and this is an area where the Museum and Libraries Archives Council (MLA) and the regional MLAs should be taking a lead.

There is a concern among public librarians about the range of new acquisitions that they will be able to buy, following the publication in July 2005 of the Department for Culture, Media and Sport/MLA report *Public Libraries: Efficiency and Stock Supply.*[5] Will this report lead to the stock of public libraries becoming more uniform? This would mean that obtaining items of limited interest would become more difficult. There used to be an expectation that public libraries would stock a wide range of material on a regional basis. For example, libraries belonging to the South West Regional Library System used to have a subject specialisation agreement for non-fiction, and another agreement for fiction. It may be difficult to maintain and justify these agreements if the most important measure of the worth of a book is the number of times it has been lent.

Organisational structure

IDS cannot be considered in isolation from developments in education, publishing, local government reorganisation and central government policy. All these have played a part in the way in which IDS has been organised in the past and they will continue to do so. There is a tension between the centralised model of IDS, based on the BL, and a decentralised model using regional library services, distributed resources and union catalogues. The organisational structure reflects this tension. IDS projects are funded from a variety of sources and we cannot expect government support for all of them. However, improving communication between all the different organisations involved and agreeing priorities would give a better framework for the development of IDS services. There has always been a strong instinct for co-operation among IDS practitioners, and we hope that future systems will build on it.

Rising expectations

People using IDS expect more and more from their library and information services. Many will be able to access sources of information from all over the world via the Web, and be aware of books published all over the globe. They know how rapidly Internet shops can supply goods, and will expect a similar service from IDS. They will become impatient of bureaucratic barriers to access and look for a seamless path from requesting an item to its arrival. IDS staff will need to focus on ways of harnessing technology to improve the service they can offer to their readers, within the limitations imposed by copyright regulations, institutional complexities and financial limitations.

Conclusion

The future is about change. Some things will remain the same; there will still be a need for lending books and sending copies. Print will still be important even though the amount of material available electronically grows. IDS librarians will find that they are adding to their services rather than losing the need for their existence. Researchers will not always have the time to search for the information they require, and may be glad to have the support of IDS librarians in finding it for them. Instead of being given specific references to locate, IDS librarians will be asked to find information on a topic and need to discover quality information from all that is available.

This is why it is important for IDS librarians to take charge of their own development. The future will bring challenges and the need to develop new skills, and we must be ready to respond. Providing a service to our users has always been the primary focus for IDS librarians. This will not change, even if the ways in which that service is delivered are transformed.

Notes

1. *http://www.sherpa.ac.uk/* [accessed 3 September 2005].
2. There is a list, the SHERPA/RoMEO Publishers Copyright Listings, on the SHERPA website at *http://www.sherpa.ac.uk/romeo.php* [accessed 3 September 2005].
3. There is a list at *http://www.doaj.org./* [accessed 3 September 2005].
4. *http://direct.bl.uk/bld/Home.do* [accessed 3 September 2005].
5. The report can be accessed from *http://www.mla.gov.uk/information/publications/00pubs.asp* [accessed 4 October 2005].

Glossary

Abbreviations

ASP: Application service provider

AULIC: Avon University Libraries in Co-operation

BL: British Library

BLCMP: Birmingham Libraries Cooperative Mechanisation Project (now TALIS)

BLIC: British Library Integrated Catalogue (BL online catalogue from 2005)

BLDSC: British Library Document Supply Centre

BLLD: British Library Lending Division

BLPC: British Library Public Catalogue (BL online catalogue 1997– 2005)

BNB: British National Bibliography

BUCOP: *British Union Catalogue of Periodicals*

BUFVC: British Universities Film and Video Council

CALIM: Consortium of Academic Libraries in Manchester, now part of NoWAL

CDPA: Copyright, Designs and Patents Act 1988

CILIP: Chartered Institute of Library and Information Professionals

CIPFA: Chartered Institute of Public Finance and Accountancy

COLICO: Committee on Library Co-operation in Ireland

COM: Computer Output Microform

Conarls: Circle of Officers of National & Regional Library Systems

COPAC: CURL Online Public Access Catalogue

CURL: Consortium of Research Libraries

DCB: Direct Consortia Borrowing

DCMS: Department for Culture, Media and Sport

DfES: Department for Education and Skills

DOI: Digital Object Identifier

DRM: Digital Rights Management

EASY: Electronic Article SupplY
e-journals: Electronic journals
EMMLAC: East Midlands Museums Libraries and Archives Council
ERA: Educational Recording Agency
FDI: Fretwell Downing Informatics
FE: Further Education
FIL: Forum for Interlending & Information Delivery
GLASS: Greater London Audio Specialisation Scheme
HE: Higher Education
IAML: International Association of Music Libraries, Archives and Documentation: Centres
IDS: Interlending and Document Supply
IFLA: International Federation of Library Associations
ILMS: Integrated Library Management System
ISBN: International Standard Book Number
ISSN: International Standard Serial Number
JANET: The Joint Academic Network – for the HE, FE and research community in the UK
JISC: Joint Information Services Committee – for the UK HE community
KVK: Karlsruhe Virtual Catalogue
LACA: Libraries and Archives Copyright Alliance
LASER: London & South Eastern library Region
LIHNN: Libraries and Information for Health Network Northwest
LIP: Library and Information Plan
LISA: *Library and Information Science Abstracts*
LISU: Library & Information Statistics Unit, based at Loughborough University
LKDN: Library and Knowledge Development Network (National Health Service)
LLDA: London Libraries Development Agency
LLU: London Lending Unit of the Department of Scientific & Industrial Research
LMS: Library Management System
LNW: Libraries North West
MLA: Museums, Libraries and Archives Council (formerly Re:Source)
MLA: Modern Language Association of America
NCL: National Central Library
NEMLAC: North East Museums Libraries and Archives Council
NESLI: National Electronic Site Licence Initiative
NFIP: National Forum for Information Planning and Co-operation

NHS: National Health Service
NLL: National Lending Library
NLLST: National Lending Library for Science & Technology
NLS: National Library of Scotland
NLW: National Library of Wales
NoWAL: North West Academic Libraries consortium
OPAC: Online Public Access Catalogue
PDF: Portable Document Format (for sending documents electronically)
PLSS: Public Library Service Standards
PSLI: Pilot Site Licensing Initiative
RDA: Regional Development Agency
RFP: Request for Proposal (in tendering for LMS contracts)
RLG: Research Libraries Group (US)
RLS: Regional Library Service/System
SCL: Society of Chief Librarians – public libraries in England and Wales
SCONUL: Society of College, National and University Libraries
SED: Secure Electronic Delivery (from the British Library)
SEMLAC: South East Museums Libraries and Archives Council
SI: Statutory Instrument
SILLR: Scottish Inter Library Loan Rate (charging scheme)
SML: Science Museum Library
SUNCAT: Serials Union Catalogue
SWMLAC: South West Museums Libraries and Archives Council
SWRLIN: South West Regional Library and Information Network (Health)
SWRLS: South Western Regional Library Service
TCR: The Combined Regions – a collaboration of RLSs that provide data for UnityWeb
TIFF: Tagged Image File Format (for sending documents electronically)
TRILT: Television and Radio Index for Learning and Teaching
UKCS: United Kingdom Core Specification
VIPs: Visually Impaired Persons
WiLL: What's in London Libraries – information and union catalogue from the London Libraries Development Agency
WWS: Worldwide Search service provided by the BL
YLI: Yorkshire Libraries and Information

Definitions

Ariel: Software developed by RLG, initially available free-of-charge, enabling libraries to send and receive articles electronically

Bee Aware: Campaign to promote interlending of alternative format materials for visually impaired and print-denied people

Co-East: Partnership bringing together libraries in the East of England in a discovery to delivery (D2D) network

Co-South: Consortium of public library authorities in the south of England (Hampshire, Isle of Wight, Portsmouth and Southampton)

DOCUSEND: Electronic document supply project

The DX: Formerly HaysDX. A courier service which transports books around the UK on behalf of members of many RLSs

BOPAC: Experimental Z39.50 union catalogue

CAIRNS: Scottish libraries' union catalogue

F4F: *Framework for the future: libraries, learning and information in the next decade.* DCMS strategic framework for public libraries, published 2003

FOURSITE: Foursite Consortium covers Bath & North East Somerset, North Somerset, South Gloucestershire and Somerset public libraries; expanding to include Bristol Public Library

HATRICS: Library and Information Plan for Hampshire and southern England

ILLOS: An IDS management system developed at Lancaster University

Inside: The British Library's Electronic Table of Contents service

INSPIRE: A government project aiming to create 'a seamless cross-sectoral pathway for learners across public, academic and national libraries'

ISO-ILL: An international standard for IDS work for ISO-ILL-compliant systems, with the technical definition of messages and rules on how they are to be used.

LAMDA: London/Manchester Document Delivery – project ended 2005. Members created a serials union catalogue which they used to request and provide articles to each other electronically, using Ariel

LinkUK: An IDS management system based on the V3.Web union catalogue, now owned by OCLC PICA

Lis-ill: An email list for IDS staff

M25: Consortium of HE and research libraries in South East England; produces a serials union list and a Z39.50 union catalogue

MIMAS: National data centre run by Manchester University for the UK HE, FE and research sectors, which provides a large number of networked services

OCLC PICA: An international library co-operative which offers a range of services, including IDS management and access to Worldcat

REVEAL: Database of publications in alternative formats for VIPs

RIDING: Z39.50 union catalogue which covers libraries in Yorkshire, Humberside and elsewhere.

RLG/SHARES: An international cross-sectoral IDS service run by RLG; some UK university libraries are members

SINTO 2000: Library and Information Plan for Sheffield area

TALIS: Talis Information Limited provides a range of products and services for public and academic libraries, including UnityWeb (until spring 2006)

UnityWeb: An online union catalogue and ILL requesting service, currently provided by TCR and TALIS

WILIP: Wider Libraries Initiative, part of the MLA

WISDOM: System connecting OPACs of a number of public libraries in South West England

Worldcat: Union catalogue; US and worldwide, available on subscription via OCLC, JISC, LinkUK and other services

Z39.50: An international standard for communication between computer systems, particularly important for bibliographic data

ZETOC: BL Electronic Table of Contents database used by the UK FE and HE sector, as well as the National Health Service

Index

Tables and figures are indicated by t, f respectively. Italics are used for publications and databases.